D1233455

# THE PRESIDENTIAL VETO

SUNY Series in Leadership Studies
Barbara Kellerman, Editor

# THE PRESIDENTIAL VETO

## Touchstone of The American Presidency

Robert J. Spitzer

with a Foreword by

Louis Fisher

State University of New York Press

Published by
State University of New York Press, Albany



Printed in the United States of America



For information, address State University of New York
Press, State University Plaza, Albany, N.Y., 12246

**Library of Congress Cataloging-in-Publication Data**

Spitzer, Robert J., 1953–
The presidential veto. Touchstone of
the American presidency
(SUNY series in leadership studies)
Bibliography: p.
1. Veto—United States—History. I. Title.
II. Series.
JK586.S67 1988 353.03'72 88-2119
ISBN 0-88706-802-2
ISBN 0-88706-803-0 (pbk.)

10 9 8 7 6 5 4 3 2 1

*Dedication*

to

Shannon Murphy, Karen Spitzer, Steven Spitzer, and Jason Popa,
the molders of the Constitution's tricentennial

# CONTENTS

# ACKNOWLEDGMENTS

The research resulting in this book was aided by several sources. This work was supported in part by a summer stipend grant from the National Endowment for the Humanities, and by a research grant from the SUNY College at Cortland Faculty Research Program. The thinking that follows benefited from the opportunity to present papers at conferences sponsored by the Northeastern Political Science Association, the National Bicentennial Conference on the American Presidency, and the American Political Science Association.

I owe special thanks to Thornton O'glove of the Reporting Research Corporation for his interest in the veto and resultant research suggestions and support, SUNY Press Leadership Series Editor Barbara Kellermen of Fairleigh Dickinson University for her faith and interest in this project, and Peggy Gifford, SUNY Press editor, for her promptness, efficiency and interest. Two former undergraduate students as SUNY Cortland, Pam Klein and Jim Cullen, both provided important background research.

In addition, my thanks to Peggy Murphy, Lori Padavona, Ron King of Cornell University, Lou Fisher of the Congressional Research Service, Library of Congress, Morris Ogul of the University of Pittsburgh, Jim Pfiffner of George Mason University, Stephen J. Wayne of George Washington University, John K. White of SUNY Potsdam, Pam O'Connell and Shary Guingo. As always, I reserve special gratitude to my first and best mentors, Bill and Jinny Spitzer.

# FOREWORD

One of the many virtues of this book is its commitment to public law, an approach that is especially timely and appropriate in this year of the bicentennial of the Constitution. Robert Spitzer has selected a key instrument of presidential power and studied its origin, purpose, development, and current use. In doing so, he exploits all the tools available to his profession: history, law, philosophy, economics, and political analysis.

Spitzer recaptures the purpose of political science when it emerged as a university discipline in the 1880s. The study was to be indisciplinary, integrating the findings of other systems to shed new light on political phenomena. The first graduate school of political science in America, set up at Columbia College in 1880, was grounded in history, law, and philosophy. America's first journal of political science, *Political Science Quarterly,* chose for its subtitle *A Review Devoted to the Historical, Statistical and Comparative Study of Politics, Economics and Public Law.* When the American Political Science Association was established in 1903, it committed itself to the "scientific study of Politics, Public Law, Administration and Diplomacy."

This is the tradition that Spitzer reawakens. Clearly, institutional and constitutional dimensions are important to him. What powers did the framers choose? For what purpose? With what limits? How does the veto fit into the overall vision of the Constitution? These are some of the questions that motivate this book.

Unfortunately, the discipline of political science has narrowed in recent years to focus increasingly on informal powers, persuasion, behavior, skills, and personality. These are valuable qualities, but not at the cost of ignoring powers expressly granted by the Constitution.

Pushed into the background, if not off the picture, have been the formal powers of government. As Spitzer correctly notes, "Despite being one of the few clearly enumerated powers of the president in the Constitution, the veto has, in many ways, been overlooked as a central and important presidential power." Again he observes: "no modern, comprehensive, analytical work on the veto exists."

Contemporary attitudes are illustrated quite nicely by the following remark of Walter Mondale in 1980: "If you asked me, if I had to give up one—the opportunity to get on the evening news or the veto power, I think I'd throw the veto power away." Of course there is no need to choose between an appearance on television and the exercise of the veto. They can be complementary powers, and generally are.

Spitzer's contribution is to study a core power of the presidency from many perspectives. He takes the subject as it is and where it naturally leads, rather than artificially presenting isolated segments. He selects the veto because it is central in maintaining the system of checks and balances, the integrity of the president's office, and the coequality between the executive and legislative branches.

The book contains an exceptionally pentrating review of the origins of the veto in Roman and British times, its adoption at the Philadelphia Convention, and the many disputes and controversies over the use of the veto. Spitzer preserves some of the most scathing language ever used in congressional debate: After one of Tyler's vetoes, a member of Congress called the president a "stupid yet perfidious devil amongst those cast out of heaven," adding that Tyler was, moreover, a "lewd spirit" and a traitor comparable to Judas Iscariot. Such are the passions stirred by the veto.

Not only does Spitzer bring the subject up to date, he argues persuasively that the veto power is an integral part of the modern strong presidency. Many of the major collisions between the president and Congress involve the decision to invoke (or the threat to invoke) the veto power. President Nixon used the veto power against the War Powers Resolution of 1973, which was passed over his veto. He used it against restrictive language that challenged his right to continue the war in Vietnam. The frequency of Ford's vetoes raised questions at the time, particularly whether an 'accidental president' could use the powers of that office as vigorously as someone elected by the people.

The veto looms large in confrontations over budget policy and foreign policy. An example is the use of the veto by President Reagan to protect his decision to send arms to Saudi Arabia. Even though his veto was sustained, Reagan made significant concessions on the weapons package to avoid an override.

If the general veto is neglected, almost completely ignored are two derivative powers: the pocket veto and the proposed item veto. The latter has become prominent because of the advocacy by President Reagan, who urges Congress each year to grant him the power to strike items from appropriations bills. At one time a sleepy constitutional issue, the item veto has been the subject of numerous hearings and spirited floor debate.

Spitzer devotes separate chapters to the pocket veto and the item veto, carefully analyzing their mechanics, the legal fights, and the political accommodations entered into by Congress and the president. For the item veto, Spitzer takes special care in examining the use of this power by governors. He then judges whether this model from the states has any application to the president and the national government. His findings should give pause to those who would grant this power to the president, whether by constitutional amendment or by statute.

This is a rich and illuminating work, giving us a deeper understanding of a central instrument of political power. The delivery is lucid and the coverage is comprehensive. I hope that Spitzer's efforts will encourage others to study the constitutional powers of the three branches: why they were included, what has come of them, and how they relate to one another.

Louis Fisher
Congressional Research Service
Library of Congress
Washington, D.C.

# INTRODUCTION

Nineteen eighty-seven began as a year of confrontation for President Ronald Reagan. In January, Congress overrode Reagan's veto of an $18 billion clean water bill, enacted earlier that month. The prompt override was provoked by the president's pocket veto of the same bill the previous November, when both houses of Congress passed the bill overwhelmingly.

Reagan's next significant legislative endeavor was his March veto of an $87.9 billion highway and mass transit funding bill that included a provision to raise the speed limit on rural interstate highways to sixty-five miles per hour. Although he favored the move to raise the speed limit, Reagan objected that the bill cost a budget-busting $10 billion more than he favored. In addition, the bill included 152 special "demonstration projects"—highway construction projects that, in many cases, were planned for the districts of influential members of Congress. In a radio address, Reagan claimed the bill was "loaded with pork barrel projects. I haven't seen so much lard," he said, "since I handed out blue ribbons at the Iowa State Fair" (*New York Times,* March 29, 1987).

The veto of the highway bill was considered a pivotal act for the president. Although the bill passed overwhelmingly in the House and handily in the Senate (79–17), Reagan launched a strong drive to uphold his veto, concentrating his efforts on the somewhat more receptive Senate. The political import of the veto was acknowledged by the president's spokesman, who admitted that a defeat "could sidetrack Mr. Reagan's political recovery from the damaging disclosures about the Iran arms deal" (*New York Times,* March 24, 1987). The risk was such that Reagan's chief of staff, former Senator Howard Baker, urged the president to back away from the veto, and Republican Senate leader Robert Dole admitted that "the stakes are very high for the President." Vermont Republican Senator Robert T. Stafford announced his support for Reagan's veto (abandoning his previous support for the bill) and considered the sustaining of the veto to be "critical to his [Reagan's] re-emergence as an active and powerful President." Democratic Senator George Mitchell considered the veto to be a grave mistake, as "it would poison chances for cooperation between the [executive and legislative] branches." White House staff recognized that the veto "could set the terms for future battles over the Federal budget and other domestic spending bills" (*New York Times,* March 25, 1987). One news analyst called the veto fight "a crucial test of his [the president's] leadership" (*New York Times,* April 1, 1987).

In this battle with Congress, Reagan's efforts (including an unusual in-person, eleventh-hour plea to Senate Republicans) fell short. The House overrode the veto easily, and the Senate did so by a 67–33 vote on April 2.

As emphasized by the comments of key actors, this veto represented a critical political struggle for the president. And as this book will argue, the presidential veto power itself is crucial to the presidency. Yet, though the importance of the veto is often noted, this importance is hardly ever examined. Only two book-length treatments of the veto power exist up to the time of this writing: The first, remarkably incisive and analytical for its time, has not been updated since its publication in 1890 (Mason), and the second is not an analysis but a historical description of bills vetoed up to 1945 (Jackson, 1967). In short, no modern, comprehensive, analytical work on the veto exists.

The aim of this work is to not only fill that gap, however, but also to promote an important argument about the veto and the presidency: The rise of the veto power, from the administration of the first chief executive, is symptomatic of the rise of the modern strong presidency, and indeed has also been a major building-presidency tool. Related closely to this argument is the observation that veto conflicts over the last two hundred years display characteristic similarities, despite numerous historical and other changes. The political tangle over Reagan's veto of the highway bill illustrates traits associated with veto use throughout our history. Some of these traits are: the centrality of the veto to presidential-congressional relations; the importance of "riders"; the importance of the president's political skills and strength (both perceived and actual); the political risks associated with a veto strategy; the veto's plebiscitary value; and the raising of pork barrel and budget-cutting issues.

The importance of the veto is accompanied by an irony as well—namely, that the veto's utility to the president did and does lie at least partly with his ability to use it as a mode of appealing directly to (and on behalf of) the people, despite the fact that the power is monarchical in origin and antimajoritarian in nature. Alexander Hamilton's advocacy of a strong veto (patterned after that of British monarchs) for the president at the Federal Convention was symptomatic of what Hartz (1955) identifies as "capitalist Whiggery" (89) and "Hamiltonian elitism," (16) characterized by a fear of democracy.

*Every Bill which shall have passed the House of Representatives and the Senate, shall, before it becomes a Law, be presented to the President of the United States; If he approves he shall sign it, but if not he shall return it, with his Objections to that House in which it shall have originated, who shall enter the Objections at large on their Journal, and proceed to reconsider it. If after such Reconsideration two thirds of that House shall agree to pass the Bill, it shall be sent, together with the Objections, to the other House, by which it shall likewise be reconsidered, and if approved by two thirds of that House, it shall become a Law. But in all such Cases the Votes of both Houses shall be determined by yeas and Nays, and the Names of the Persons voting for and against the Bill shall be entered on the Journal of each House respectively. If any Bill shall not be returned by the President within ten Days (Sundays excepted) after it shall have been presented to him, the Same shall be a Law, in like Manner as if he had signed it, unless the Congress by their Adjournment prevent its Return, in which Case it shall not be a Law.*

*Every Order, Resolution, or Vote to which the Concurrence of the Senate and House of Representatives may be necessary (except on a question of Adjournment) shall be presented to the President of the United States; and before the Same shall take Effect, shall be approved by him, or, being disapproved by him, shall be repassed by two thirds of the Senate and House of Representatives, according to the Rules and Limitations prescribed in the Case of a Bill.*

*Article I, Section 7*
*United States Constitution*

# 1
# The Creation of the Veto

*The most important of all the checks and balances is, of course, the presidential veto. . . .*

James L. Sundquist (1986)

The study of the presidential veto begins with its roots. To understand the antecedents and construction of this key presidential power is to understand much about that power (and the presidency) today. Thus, we begin with a detailed history of the veto power from ancient Rome to the completion of the Constitution. But this book also goes beyond the history of the veto, however, to argue two important points: (1) The veto power, in and of itself, possesses certain traits that transcend its application to American government: and (2) the application and rise of the presidential veto is symptomatic of the rise of the modern strong presidency. In short, perspectives on the presidential veto reflect perspectives on the presidency itself.

## Antecedents of the veto

The veto is a power that transcends the American experience. It is thus important to understand its antecedents, not only because the American founders were influenced by this history, but also because the very nature of the veto power, as it can be traced through history, may be revealed in ways useful to the study of the presidential veto.

### *Ancient Rome*

The *Oxford English Dictionary* identifies the word *veto* as deriving from Latin meaning 'I forbid.' In the sixth century B.C., early in the

Roman Republic, the veto (called *intercessio*) was adopted as a device by Roman tribunes to protect the interests of the plebeians (citizens whose interests the tribunes represented) against the encroachments of the patricians. A tribunal *intercessio* was an absolute veto that could block any magisterial act—that is, an act passed by the patrician-dominated senate (where tribunes also served) and accepted by the consuls and other magistrates—as long as it affected plebeians. The veto could also preclude bringing a bill before the plebeian assembly. A bill vetoed in the senate could still pass through, but it lacked the force of law and served only as an expression of opinion (Buckland, 1925: 1–2; Jolowicz, 1967: 10–13).

As the Roman Republic evolved, the plebeians' struggle with the patricians for political and economic equality was greatly facilitated by the veto power, though the use of the veto also contributed to a certain degree of institutional paralysis and anarchy (Jolowicz, 1967: 12–13). Veto power was not limited to the tribunes, however. Patrician representatives had similar power, as did the two consuls—the highest elected offices of the Roman Republic. The consuls' powers were kingly, extending to all matters except religion. They operated on the principle of 'colleagueship,' meaning quite simply that mutual cooperation was necessary for decisionmaking in most matters. When the two consuls could not agree, either could invoke the *intercessio,* vetoing the action of the other and leaving matters as they were. In the Roman magistracy, power was seen as twofold: (1) affirmative management of state affairs; and (2) restraint of the actions of magistrates of equivalent or inferior rank. While the highest leaders possessed both types of power, tribunes were limited mostly to the veto. Nevertheless, through the tribunes' use of this power, plebeians gained important concessions (*Encyclopaedia Britannica,* 1910–11: 14). As Rome evolved, the significance of the politics of *intercessio* was overshadowed by the return of the monarchy and increasingly autocratic control by the Caesars (Jolowicz, 1967: 43–45).

### *The veto in Europe*

The veto continued in Europe as one of many Roman vestiges left to subsequent cultures. In 1652, the imperial diet of the Kingdom of Poland allowed for the right of a deputy to block a decision approved of by the other members through the utterance of the phrase

*Nie pozwalam,* or "I do not permit it." In 1789, the French king was given a "suspensory veto" by the National Assembly—that is, one subject to override "if the Assembly persisted in its resolution." The French Revolution came the same year and brought an end not only to the veto but the king as well. The Spanish Constitution of 1812 adopted a similar qualified veto, saying that the king might return a bill twice that had been presented to him by two sessions of the Cortes. If the same bill were presented a third time, however, he could not then refuse assent. This procedure was also adopted for the Norwegian monarch in that country's constitution of 1814 (*Encyclopaedia Britannica,* 1910–11: 14).

## The English tradition

The centrality of the monarch to the English lawmaking process was related directly to his or her use of the veto: Its use reflected the monarch's relations with Parliament. To appreciate this assertion more fully, one must begin with two important observations. First, the English king was initially the supreme lawmaking authority, though his authority was usually exercised through noblemen (Mason, 1890: 12; Beard, 1914: 613; Dicey, 1927: 48). Second, the Parliament, which today holds this authority, was a creation of the monarch (Chrimes, 1965: 13). Even though monarchs have played no important role in lawmaking in the last two centuries, they have been considered members of Parliament, because it "is in theory [the king's] Great Council" (Bryce, 1891, I: 52–53).

During and after the eleventh-century Norman conquest of England, kingly powers were enhanced. The Parliament of the time maintained formal power over lawmaking, but substantively, the legislative agenda was controlled by the king. He generally presented matters to Parliament, but even then, his final approval was necessary to enact legislation. And even these formalities were sometimes swept aside when the king issued proclamations (Mason, 1890: 12–13).

Yet Parliament increasingly resented kingly creation of laws, and as its power and the democratic urge grew, so too did its influence on lawmaking. Beginning about the fourteenth century, the House of Commons began petitioning monarchs to make laws on particular subjects. The monarchs could exceed parliamentary requests, however, and often issued laws that bore no relation to the petitions presented. Commons petitions then became more precise, and pressure on monarchs to conform increased. By the sixteenth century, the Crown was reduced to either accepting or rejecting what had become an 'act of Parliament.' Thus Mason writes: "The veto is a remnant of the more extensive legislative power formerly held by the English kings" (Mason, 1890: 14–15; also Beard, 1914: 613).

Even after parliamentary acquisition of lawmaking, the Crown still maintained parallel power through 'royal legislation,' also called 'ordinances' and 'proclamations' (Dicey, 1927, 48–49). Their initial purpose was to enforce laws, yet proclamations were soon adapted by monarchs to create law (Mason, 1890: 13). In 1539, Henry VIII formally granted to the British monarch this authority in the Act Thirty-One, which said that such monarchical declarations "shall be observed as though they were made by Act of Parliament" (Dicey, 1927: 49)—a definition remarkably similar to that of presidential executive orders. Yet clearly such monarchical discretion was at odds with the rule of law and democratic values, and the law was repealed during the reign of Henry's successor, Edward VI. Monarchs continued to issue proclamations, however, until a parliamentary prohibition in 1766 (Mason, 1890: 13).

The atrophy of kingly lawmaking left only the veto as a weapon against Parliament. What was once an integral aspect of lawmaking became simply a power to prevent. The use of the veto was invoked with the phrase *le roi s'avisera* ("The king will consider it"); approval of a bill was *le roi le vult* ("The king wishes it") (Chrimes, 1965: 13). Both phrases were remnants of the time when French was the language of the Court.

The veto continued to be employed, but, being absolute in nature, it also aroused progressively greater passions as time passed. Queen Elizabeth I was not reluctant to veto; in 1597, for example, she approved forty-three bills, but vetoed forty-seven. Her successor, James I, was more frugal with his power: At the end of the 1606 session, he observed that his restraint in vetoing no bills that year was explainable "as a special token of grace and favour, being a matter unusual to pass all acts without exception" (Hearn, 1867: 60). Charles I provoked considerable ire with his veto of a militia bill and other measures, which by at least one account was a direct cause of the

1643 revolution (Mason, 1890: 16). Parliament subsequently enacted the militia bill despite the veto.[1]

The veto continued to be used, even after the Revolution of 1688, though with even greater circumspection. William III invoked the veto at least six times (Mason, 1890: 16, n.6), "always exciting thereby some indignation on the part of parliament" (Adams, 1934: 373) even though the vetoes involved bills which "infringed upon some part of the prerogative or seemed to him of doubtful expedience" (Hearn, 1867: 60). His successor, Queen Anne, employed the royal veto for the last time on March 11, 1707. The bill in question was a measure to arm the Scottish militia. The bill aroused little interest until, on the day it was to be signed, news arrived that the French were sailing to Scotland. Anne quickly had broad support for the veto, as the loyalty of the Scots was questionable, and a veto was the most expeditious way to kill the bill (Hearn, 1867: 61).

If the veto became a relic of a bygone era, so too did a companion power—impeachment. As the king could 'bash' the Parliament with the veto, so too could Parliament 'bash' the king with impeachment. By impeachment, Parliament could accuse royal officials—including the monarch—of misconduct, and try them on such charges. According to one expert on the British constitution, these two powers represented "conflict of the old sort between executive and legislature" (Adams, 1934: 373). As if to verify the symmetry between the veto and impeachment, impeachment was also abandoned in the eighteenth century.

The typical explanation for the fact that British monarchs ceased to apply the veto is simply that its absolute nature discouraged its use (e.g., Curtis, 1859, II: 266; Zinn, 1951: 3; Federalist #73, 1961; Clineburg, 1966: 734). Yet closer scrutiny reveals that the veto issue was not by any means dead after 1707.

First, as is well known, veto power continued to be used with regularity over acts of American colonial legislatures, either by colonial governors, Parliament, or the monarch through his or her ministers. The first two complaints lodged against George III in the Declaration of Independence—that "He has refused his Assent to Laws, the most wholesome and necessary for the public Good" and that "He has forbidden his Governors to pass Laws of immediate and pressing Importance"—are complaints against the use of the veto. As Moe (1987: 418) notes, however, the colonists' resentment was not directed at the idea of the kingly negative, but rather at "the arbitrary and detailed nature of the negative in practice." Despite the adverse affect this had on British-American relations, monarchical vetoes over measures enacted in other British colonies continued into the twentieth century, though the veto's exercise was much less frequent by then (Dicey, 1927: 111–15).

Second, as is not so well known, the fall of the royal veto into disuse is not explainable solely or even principally by the fear that it was too great a power. Rather, it is clear that, at least in the eighteenth century, royal influence (exercised through the king or his ministers) could alter or defeat a bill before it was passed, obviating the need to use the veto. In fact, concern that the king's influence was excessive prompted various measures to limit it—in particular, legislation written into a Bill for Economic Reform, pushed by Edmund Burke, was designed to eliminate various lucrative sinecures used by the king to buy votes (Taswell-Langmead, 1946: 717). Even during the Stuart era of the seventeenth century, the monarchs were able to avoid wider use of the veto because, according to one British historian, they "lightly assented to bills that they never intended to observe" (Hearn, 1867: 60).

Moreover, many have argued that the royal veto, or threat of a royal veto, has continued to play a role in British politics.[2] In 1852, Disraeli said that he thought the right of the crown to refuse assent to legislation "was still outstanding" (Jennings, 1959: 395). During a fierce political battle over the Home Rule Bill in the period 1912–14, some argued that George V could refuse his assent (Jennings, 1959: 395). "It was assumed by the King throughout that he had not only the legal power but the constitutional right to refuse assent" (Jennings, 1959: 400). At the same time, the king was acutely aware that to do so would result in the resignation of ministers, dissolution of Parliament and wide-ranging debate over the power of the crown. A veto could only be palatable politically if used on direct advice from political leaders (Jennings, 1959: 300). Still, the veto specter was part of the public debate, as was the ability of monarchs to avoid a possible veto confrontation by applying political pressure (Watson, 1910, I: 362, n.32).

During the home rule controversy, British constitutional expert Albert V. Dicey wrote a letter to the *Times* (September 15, 1913) in which he argued that the veto had become obsolete simply because any circumstances that gave it rise could be more cleanly dealt with by dissolution of Parliament. Dicey went on to quote with approval Edmund Burke (writing 150 years previously):

> The King's negative to Bills is one of the most undisputed of the Royal prerogatives, and it extends to all cases whatsoever. . . . But it is not the propriety of the exercise which is in question. Its repose may be the preservation of its existence, and its existence may be the means of saving the Constitution itself on an occasion worthy of bringing it forth. (Jennings, 1959: 545)

One other trait of the British monarchical veto warrants mention. For a time, its use was encouraged for a reason remarkably similar to that heard today about the presidential veto. During the latter part of the seventeenth century, the House of Commons resorted to a practice referred to by the British as "tacking." Based on the rule that the House of Lords could not amend a money bill, the Commons would include in such bills what we refer to as "riders"—nongermane amendments—which would not otherwise be acceptable to the Lords, so that they would be obliged to accept or reject such a bill *in toto.* This tacking first occurred in 1667. The following year, Charles II announced that he would veto any such bill. Still, tacking was used successfully in 1692, 1698, and 1701. The practice fell into disuse in the eighteenth century, as there was a "wide sense of [it] being a misuse of technicalities for the purpose of evading a recognised constitutional principle" (Taswell-Langmead, 1946: 613–14).

Though this examination of the British veto takes us past the writing of the American Constitution, it is important for at least two reasons. First, British practice was much on the minds of the founding fathers in constructing our Constitution, as seen in public debate and documents of the time. Second, the consequences of use of the veto as a political tool in Britain (despite its use by a hereditary monarch) are very similar to the political consequences of the American veto: Its use in Britain was considered a politically extreme and controversial act; it was viewed as a weapon of last resort; it was understood to be a legislative power; it intertwined with the issue of tacking; and, finally and perhaps most important, its perceived power was symptomatic of the political jockeying between the executive and legislative branches.

## The veto in America

The establishment of colonies in America occurred primarily through the prerogative of the British Crown, which sanctioned early colonial constitutions. As mentioned, colonial governors were appointed by the king, except for those of Connecticut and Rhode Island, which elected their governors to one-year terms. All governors possessed absolute veto powers over colonial legislation, either through charter, royal instruction, or proprietary grant, but in Maryland, the burgesses refused to recognize the gubernatorial veto. The king's absolute veto could be applied to colonial acts in any of the colonies except Connecticut and Rhode Island (charter colonies) and Maryland (a proprietary colony). Yet even in these states, royal disapproval could be transmitted through crown-appointed officials (Mason, 1890: 17; Zinn, 1951: 3).

The king not only had the veto, but used it with relative frequency, as the veto was considered a vital tool for protecting British interests. An example of this use is the Crown's veto of Virginia's attempt to limit the slave trade (Mason, 1980: 17–18). Gubernatorial vetoes were similarly odious to colonists. For example, in a 1722 bill designed to amend the Corporation of Harvard College constitution, Governor Shute vetoed the bill, then conditioned subsequent approval on the reinstatement of three corporation fellows who had been removed. The Massachusetts House balked but ultimately gave in to Shute's demand (Mason, 1890: 18, n.3). During the Federal Constitutional Convention deliberations, Benjamin Franklin described how the colonial governor extracted private perquisites in exchange for assent: "the negative of the Governor was constantly made use of to extort money. No good law whatsoever could be passed without a private bargain with him" (Farrand, 1966, I: 98–99).

### *The state experience*

Once the colonies broke free of British control, their initial response to the onerous veto was to make it unavailable to their own executives. In fact, with the exception of New York, most state constitutions were careful to subordinate the executive to the legislature (Thach, 1923: 28). Some states abandoned the governor altogether in favor of a commission.

South Carolina experimented first with the veto in its temporary constitution of 1776. It gave its governor (referred to as the President and Commander-in-Chief) an absolute veto. Yet when Governor John Rutledge actually used the power, the consequent outcry forced him to resign. In South Carolina's 1778 constitution, the veto power was eliminated (Watson, 1987: 405).

New York was the first state to permanently bestow an executive veto power. This fact, combined with the greater independence given to the governor, is explained by the larger fact that, unlike the other states, it established a strong governor in its constitution of 1777. New York did this for several reasons: the state's relative conservatism; the influence of such leaders as Jay, Livingston, and Morris; and the fact that New York delayed in finalizing its constitution, which allowed time for observation of the adverse consequences of weak executives in other states (Thach, 1923: 34–35). According to the New York Constitution, the governor would join with judges of the state supreme court and the chancellor of the court of chancery in a council of revision to assess all bills passed by the state legislature: "All bills which have passed the senate or assembly shall before they become laws be presented to the said council for the revisal and consideration" (Benton, 1888: 37). If a majority of the council shared reservations, the bill was to be returned to the chamber of origin, with the inclusion of written objections, for reconsideration. A two-thirds vote in both chambers would override the veto. If the council did not return the bill to the legislature within ten days, it automatically became law, unless the legislature adjourned for more than ten days, in which case the bill would be returned on the first day of the new session. (Within its first three years, the council of revision vetoed ten bills; in its first ten years, it vetoed fifty-eight bills [Benton, 1888: 40, 42].)[3]

Two observations warrant special mention here: These provisions bear remarkable resemblence to the veto in the federal Constitution; and the emphasis of the veto power was on reconsideration and revision of legislation, not simply blocking its passage. We will return to both of these themes later.

Later in 1777, the Vermont Constitution incorporated what was, in effect, a non-binding veto.[4] It said that "all bills of a public nature shall be first laid before the governor and council for their perusal and proposals of amendment" (Benton, 1888: 38).

In 1780, the Massachusetts Constitution gave to the governor for the first time sole "power of revision" over legislation. The provisions of the constitution pertaining to the veto, adopted in Massachusetts with little debate, were nearly identical in wording and concept to the New York Constitution, with the exceptions that the governor had only five days to consider the bill and that he could act alone.

The previously proposed Massachusetts Constitution, defeated in a state referendum in 1778, made no provision for the veto (Benton, 1888: 39, 40). It was clear that the utility and desirability of "power of revision" had been demonstrated by New York. Alexander Hamilton observed in 1780 that the council of revision's "utility has become so apparent that persons who in compiling the constitution were violent opposers of it, have from experience become its declared admirers" (Benton, 1888: 40). In the Massachusetts convention, the rationale for adopting the veto was "to preserve the laws from being unsystematical and inaccurate" and so that "due balance may be preserved in the three capital powers of government" (Benton, 1888: 41). In the succeeding ten years, the Massachusetts governor returned a total of one bill and two resolves to the legislature (Benton, 1888: 59).

### *The Articles of Confederation*

Antipathy not only to the veto power but to the very idea of a single, autonomous executive found its most naked expression in the country's first constitution, the Articles of Confederation. It made no provision for an executive. The paralytic nature of decisionmaking under the Articles was amply demonstrated by the fact that most important measures considered by the national congress required a majority of nine out of thirteen state votes for passage; proposals to amend the Articles required a unanimous vote. Thus, a single state, or group of five, could 'veto' important measures.[5] The resultant stalemates did much to prompt the call for major changes in the governing document.

## The federal convention

When the founders convened in Philadelphia in May of 1787, they faced a multitude of problems, not the least of which was the matter

of executive power. Was there to be an executive, and if so, would the executive power be held in the hands of an individual or a group? And what would be the scope of the executive's power? Central to all of these questions was the matter of the veto power.
The initial resolution of these issues was embodied in the Virginia plan, offered by Edmund Randolph, but written mostly by James Madison. It called for a single president, to be elected by the Congress for a single term (the length of which was not initially set). The president was to have a qualified veto—that is, subject to override (percent unspecified)—but it was to be exercised in concert with a council of revision, composed of "a convenient number of the National Judiciary" (Farrand, 1966, I: 21).

The Virginia plan gave the convention a fresh starting point, though the plan was changed substantially during the hot Philadelphia summer. In relation to the veto power, the options considered ran the full range from having no veto, as proposed in the New Jersey plan (which also proposed a plural executive elected by Congress [Farrand, 1966, I: 244]), to granting an absolute veto. Also, was the veto to be exercised with a council, or alone? If the veto was to be subject to override, what percent was appropriate? Should veto powers be held by anyone else in the national government? And finally, what were the founders' perceptions of the nature of this power? The resolution of these questions was central to determining whether the president would be strong or weak, dependent or independent, assertive or compliant. In this way, the story of the veto is also the story of the presidency.

### *The veto: Absolute or qualified?*

Despite the stigma surrounding the veto power, based on its use by the British, there was surprisingly little objection to incorporating the veto in some form (Mason, 1890: 20). The arguments against granting any veto to the president included these: The president was not likely to have any greater wisdom or insight than a given congressman; the veto resembled too closely a monarchical power; ultimate sovereignty rested not with the president, but with the legislature; the president's single voice ought not to supercede two houses of Congress; and the president would play a role in the legislative process anyway, obviating the need for a veto (Farrand, 1966, I: 106–110; III: 202–203).

Though these individual arguments crop up periodically throughout the proceedings, they did little to sway the convention as a whole against some kind of veto power.

Arguments were also made at various junctures to grant an absolute veto, based on the sense that the president would need such a tool to maintain his independence and strength. Foremost among those pressing this argument was Hamilton. By virtue of his advocacy of an absolute veto as the keystone of a strong executive, he was unjustly accused later of promoting monarchy (Farrand, 1913: 88). Wilson also argued for the necessity of an absolute veto: "Without such a self-defence the Legislature can at any moment sink it [the executive] into non-existence" (Farrand, 1966, I: 98). Read said that the absolute negative was "essential to the Constitution, to the preservation of liberty, and to the public welfare" (Farrand, 1966, II: 200). Hamilton pointed out that little danger of overuse of the veto existed, as even the British monarch had not used it in many years. Yet the reference to the British king backfired. Sherman argued against one man having the power to stop the will of Congress as too antimajoritarian (Farrand, 1966, I: 99).[6] Mason commented, with what must have been some sarcasm: "We are not indeed constituting a British Government, but a more dangerous monarchy, an elective one" (Farrand, 1966, I: 101). To him, the absolute veto meant, in effect, popular surrender of the rights of the people to a single leader. Butler observed, with some presentiment, that "in all countries the Executive power is in a constant course of increase"; there was, thus, legitimate concern that even a nonmonarchical executive, like England's Cromwell, could become too powerful (Farrand, 1966, I: 100).

Franklin also spoke against an absolute veto, citing the tendency of the Pennsylvania colonial governor to extort money and other perquisites (Farrand, 1966, I: 98–99). Madison spoke in favor of the efficacy of a qualified veto, arguing that the president would rarely use a veto unless he already had at least some political support in Congress (Farrand, 1966, I: 99–100). Later, Hamilton adopted a similar tack in the Federalist Papers (#73, 1961: 446) when he wrote that the qualified veto "would be less apt to offend" and "more apt to be exercised" and therefore would be "more effectual." Despite the fact that the vote on the Wilson-Hamilton proposal was decisively negative (0–10), the proposal was reintroduced several times, and decisively defeated on each occasion.[7]

The convention was less decisive on the admittedly more arbitrary question of the override percent. Early in the convention's deliberations (June 4), a two-thirds veto override was agreed on (by an 8–2 vote, without debate). In August, however, Williamson proposed that the percent be changed to three-fourths. Carrol argued that when two-thirds had been agreed to, no quorum had been set for the new Congress. But now that it had, he perceived the need to set a higher override threshold to establish "greater impediments to improper laws" (Farrand, 1966, II: 300). This, combined with a sense that presidential self-protection would be enhanced, resulted in a 6–4–1 vote for the change (Farrand, 1966, II: 299–301). A month later, however, the convention changed its mind, reverting back to two-thirds, again by Williamson's motion. Madison observed that the president was to be elected by the Congress for a single seven-year term when three-fourths had been adopted; but since that time, presidential election was changed to four years and to election by the people. There was a sense at this juncture on the part of Wilson and others that three-fourths gave too much to the president. Pinckney in particular observed that three-fourths would put too much power in the hands of the president and a handful of senators, making them capable of blocking an override attempt (Farrand, 1966, II: 586). The motion to revert to two-thirds was 6–4–1. One other fine-tuning amendment was made on August 15, when the length of time allotted for the president to sign or return a bill was increased from seven to ten days, Sundays excepted, by a vote of 9–2, apparently with no significant debate (Farrand, 1966, II: 295).

### *The council of revision proposal*

Provisions for executive power were drawn heavily from the state constitutions of New York and Massachusetts (Mason, 1890: 20–21; Farrand, 1913: 145–46; Ford, 1967: 176). Clearly, the successful operation of a council of revision in New York (Prescott and Zimmerman, 1980: 49–52) inspired the same proposal in the Randolph plan (Thach, 1923: 88). Yet it was challenged from the start, primarily on the grounds that it violated separation of powers (Federalist #73, 1961: 446–47). Gerry argued that it was "quite foreign from the nature of ye. office to make them [court justices] judges of the policy of public measures" (Farrand, 1966, I: 97–98). King argued that "the

Judges ought to be able to expound the law as it should come before them, free from the bias of having participated in its formation" (Farrand, 1966, I: 98). Ghorum pointed out that English judges possessed no similar power, and that judges "are not to be presumed to possess any peculiar knowledge of the mere policy of public measures" (Farrand, 1966, II: 73). In general, there was a strong sense among opponents of this plan that the involvement of judges in the legislative process at this or any other point would give the court, in essence, two chances to rule on a law (Farrand, 1913: 119–20).

Despite these arguments, several delegates persisted on behalf of a council of revision to share veto powers. Wilson argued that a council was needed to shore up executive power, so that both branches of government, and the people as well, might be better protected from congressional encroachments (Farrand, 1966, I: 138; II: 73). He also observed that, while judges would have the opportunity for subsequent review of legislation, they might be confronted with laws that were unjust, unwise, dangerous, and destructive, but still not unconstitutional (and thus beyond the court's power to change) (Farrand, 1966, I: 138; II: 73). Madison concurred, adding that the veto would be too weak if in the hands of the president alone. To him, the genius of the scheme of government was "to collect the wisdom of its several parts in aid of each other whenever it was necessary" (Farrand, 1966, I: 110, 144). The persistence of this debate was evidenced by the fact that four attempts (all unsuccessful) were made by Madison and Wilson to join the president and Supreme Court in the exercise of the veto. The idea of constituting a council of revision composed of the president and members of his cabinet was also floated (Farrand, 1966, II: 135), but this notion found little support. Mason said "we can hardly find worse materials out of which to create a council of revision" (Farrand, 1966, I: 111).

### *A veto over state laws*

The original Virginia Plan included provision for the Congress "to negative all laws passed by the several States, contravening in the opinion of the National Legislature the articles of Union" (Farrand, 1966, I: 21). This veto was viewed initially as instrumental to assuring that state powers be kept subordinate to federal authority, especially given recent experience under the Articles which revealed a tendency for states to encroach on federal authority (Farrand, 1966, I: 164–69). By July, however, sentiment had shifted. Sherman argued that the power was unnecessary, especially given the likelihood that state courts would not uphold state laws that contravened national law. Morris concurred, citing both the courts in general as a check and the option of federal legislation against states should the need arise. He also considered such a congressional veto to be unnecessarily harsh on the states. Madison defended the proposal as necessary to the integrity of the federal system. By one account, this veto "occupied a central place in his [Madison's] plan for extending the sphere of republican government" (Hobson, 1979: 216; also Warren, 1937: 164–71, 316–24, 512, 548). Nevertheless, the provision was excised by a vote of 3–7 (Farrand, 1966, II: 27–28).

A proposal was also floated to grant the president the power to veto state laws. Reportedly, it was moved by Madison, seconded by Pinckney, and probably supported by Hamilton (Farrand, 1966, III: 399). It was not, however, an idea that garnered much support or serious attention.

### *A power of suspension*

One effort to resolve the dispute over the veto power was proposed by Butler on June 4. Seconded by Franklin, it proposed that "the National Executive have a power to suspend any legislative act for the term of ____" (no time was specified; Farrand, 1966, I: 103). Presumably, such a power would simply have held a bill in abeyance for a given period of time without requiring an override vote, but allowing for subsequent reconsideration by Congress. Mason argued that such a power would simply be insufficient, and Gerry said that "a power of suspending might do all the mischief dreaded from the negative of useful laws; without answering the salutary purpose of checking unjust or unwise ones" (Farrand, 1966, I: 102, 104). The vote to grant suspending power was unanimous against (0–10).

### *The purpose of the veto*

Again and again in the convention's consideration of the veto power, one central theme persistently surfaced: the veto as a device of executive self-protection against encroachments of the legislature. This had indisputably been the lesson gleaned from state experiences. As Thach (1969: 53) observes, state experiences "demonstrated the necessity for the veto as a protective measure." In addition, they also showed the utility of the veto "as a means of preventing unwise legislation," and "revealed the desirability of bringing legislative business into a single whole by the executive department." In the convention, Gerry stated that the purpose of "the Revisionary power was to secure the Executive department agst. legislative encroachment" (Farrand, 1966, II: 74–75). Reflecting on state experiences, Madison observed: "Experience had proved a tendency in our governments to throw all power into the legislative vortex. The Executives of the States are in general little more than cyphers; the legislatures omnipotent" (Farrand, 1966, II: 35). Willson and Hamilton justified their proposal for granting an absolute veto by saying that "the natural operation of the Legislature will be to swallow up the Executive" (Farrand, 1966, I: 107; see also Thach, 1923: 45–46). This precise theme of tying the veto to presidential defense from legislative usurpation appears in three of the four Federalist Papers that mention the veto (1961, #51: 322–23; #66: 402; #73: 442,444), and many times later (e.g., Story, 1833, II: 347; Bryce, 1891, I: 219–20; Tocqueville, 1945, I: 126; Zinn, 1951: 5). This narrow focus on self-defense is understood, of course, to be part of the larger concern with separation of powers and checks and balances. This concern recognizes that the executive's successful participation in the government is predicated on the ability to interact and compete successfully with the other branches of government.

The concept of executive self-defense also arises with the pocket veto power. As mentioned, federal veto provisions bore close resemblance to those of Massachusetts and especially New York. Yet the one major difference between the New York and federal veto provisions was that bills vetoed within ten days of legislative adjournment in New York were held over until the legislature reconvened. A comparable presidential veto, however, is in effect an absolute veto as the bill is not returned. The reason for this change was again executive self-protection. It was feared that the Congress might decide to adjourn as a means of preventing the president from returning bills. Unable to be returned, the bills would then become law without the president's signature (Story, 1833, II: 355; *Debates in Congress,* December 5, 1833: 18). There is no indication that the founders realized the full consequences of this de facto absolute veto. This is reflected also in the storm of protest that arose later when the pocket veto was used in the nineteenth century.

### *The functions of the veto*

Based on the convention debates and discussion, it is clear that the functional application of the veto was conceived to be wide ranging. Madison summarized several purposes, including protection of other branches of government from legislative aggression, protection of the rights of the people, prevention of laws "unwise in their principle" as well as laws "incorrect in their form" (Farrand, 1966, I: 139), and to "prevent popular or factious injustice" (Farrand, 1913: 184). Hamilton made very similar arguments in Federalist #73 (1961: 442–43).

Martin talked of the veto as being used to block measures "*hastily* or *rashly* adopted" (Farrand, 1966, III: 203). Mason similarly considered it a shield against "unjust and pernicious" laws (Farrand, 1966, II: 78). The use of the veto to block laws deemed unconstitutional was a motive traced back to the veto in New York (Thach, 1967: 40–41). This precedent became part of the rationale during the federal convention as well (Story, 1833, II: 348; Farrand, 1913, 119–20; Farrand, 1966, II: 78). Writing to Jefferson in 1788, Madison said, "A revisionary power is meant as a check to precipitate, to unjust, and to unconstitutional laws" (Farrand, 1966, IV: 81). This wide array of functions becomes especially significant when examining the application of the veto by early presidents and the fierce political debate throughout the nineteenth century over the appropriate and inappropriate uses of the veto. Such an examination, however, lies beyond the scope of this chapter.

### *The nature of the veto power*

Three observations about the nature of the veto power as conceived by the founders merit particular attention. First, as with the exercise of many varieties of governmental power, the founders felt a certain ambivalence toward the veto power. One indication of this is seen in the very use—or more properly, nonuse—of the word itself. Nowhere in the Constitution does the word *veto* appear, even though the paragraph that describes it is the second longest in the document. In Farrand's *Records of the Federal Convention,* the word appears in the text no more than once or twice. During actual debates, the terms *negative, qualified negative, revisionary power, and restraining power* are all used as synonyms. In the four Federalist Papers that mention this power (#51, #66, #69, #73), the word *veto* appears but once (in #73). It is well understood that this semantic ploy was no accident, but reflected a keen awareness of the monarchical roots of this power and the resentment that its use by the king and his colonial governors had engendered in America. The use of the word was considered impolitic (Wilkinson, 1936: 108n), and the founders certainly wanted to avoid an adverse reaction from the country to a power considered essential for the president.

Second, the veto power intended for the president was understood by the founders to be a legislative power. Its inclusion in article I of the Constitution (the article that deals with legislative powers) instead of article II (which deals with presidential powers) reflects this understanding. As mentioned previously, the British monarch's exercise of the veto over parliamentary acts was considered a legislative power, and this view was accepted by the founders as well (e.g., Farrand, 1966, III: 203). More recent analysts have offered the same observation (e.g. Bryce, 1891, I: 220). "The exercise of the veto power is patently a legislative act . . . being associated with the Legislature for the special purpose of arresting its action by [the president's] disapproval" (Zinn, 1951: 6, 37).

Third, both the founders' conception of the circumstances under which the veto could be applied, and the quality of the power itself, were substantially broader than is typically realized or acknowledged. This is important partly because of the subsequent conflicts over the circumstances of veto use, which in the minds of the founders were extremely broad. Essentially, the president was free, in constitutional terms, to veto any bill that crossed his desk, as long as he stated his reasons for doing so and then returned the bill to the legislative chamber of origin. In a Committee of Detail Draft of the Constitution, written during the federal convention in July, the application of the veto was summarized by saying that a bill might be returned if "it shall appear to him [the president] improper for being passed into a Law" (Farrand, 1966, II: 167). No other circumstances were specified. It is difficult to conceive of any piece of legislation not covered by this language.

Moreover, no limitation on the frequency of veto use was prescribed. Here also, the words of the framers are often misunderstood. Federalist #73 (1961: 443–45) is often cited as evidence to support the proposition that the founders *intended* the veto to be used rarely, because of its extraordinary nature. Yet Hamilton is making a different point in this essay. He first defends the necessity of the veto as "a shield to the executive," a check against improper laws, and a check against the legislature as a whole. He then counters the objection to the veto that it imposes the president's will by virtue of his "superior wisdom" by arguing instead that the veto is justifiable because of "the supposition that the legislature will not be infallible." Though the veto might be used to block good laws as well as bad, the power is eminently defensible because it ensures more consideration in the legislative process. Hamilton then offers the political observation that the singular nature of the veto power is such that it "would generally be employed with great caution." Even the British king, Hamilton notes, showed care and restraint toward use of the veto. Such consideration would be even greater for an elected executive who shares governing authority. In fact, Hamilton suggests, the principal concern would likely be that the veto would be used too rarely, not too often. The president would be constrained in veto use by its effects on "the power of his office" and "the sanction of his constituents." Hamilton's defense of the veto represents a prediction *of its likely use,* not a prescription *for its intended use.* Yet as recently as the last decade, President Ford was criticized for his frequent and wide-ranging use of the veto (Pyle and Pious, 1984: 220).

In terms of the quality of the veto power itself, the typical consideration of it today is that it is simply a power to block—a power of refusal, purely negative in nature. Though the founders spoke of "the negative," the federal debates emphasized not so much its negative nature, as its revisionary nature—a tool for the reconsideration and/or revision of legislation (e.g., Farrand, 1966, II: 73–79, 161, 568–69; III: 133, 385).[8] This is seen in both the ability of Congress to override the veto (unlike the absolute veto) and in the constitutional requirement that the president must state his objections in writing (see Benton, 1888: 35–36). These two stipulations underscore a role for the president in actively shaping legislation by use of the veto, though this is not the only presidential role in the lawmaking process described in the Constitution. This revisionary, constructive component has been mostly lost in two hundred years of acrimonious political squabbling over the veto.

Up until the final draft of the Constitution, the veto paragraph was worded this way (as late as September 10, seven days before the conclusion of the convention on September 17):

> Every bill . . . shall, before it become a law, be presented to the President of the United States, *for his revision;* if, *upon such revision,* he approve of it he shall signify his approbation by signing it: But if upon such revision it shall appear to him improper, for being passed into a law, he shall return it, together with his objections against it, to that House in which it shall have originated. . . . (Farrand, 1966, II: 568–69; emphasis added)

The draft does not say simply, as it might have, that the president may, at his discretion, employ the negative. The final changes in the wording of this paragraph involved grammatical weeding and paring. No debate on dropping the revisionary wording appears in the *Records.* In a letter written to Jefferson, who had been in Europe during the convention, Madison talked of the veto power in this way:

> Some contended for an absolute negative, as the only possible mean of reducing to practice the theory of a free Government which forbids a mixture of the Legislative & Executive powers. Others would be content with a revisionary power, to be overruled by three fourths of both Houses. It was warmly urged that the judiciary department should be associated in the revision. The idea of some was that a separate revision should be given to the two departments—that if either objected two thirds, if both, three fourths, should be necessary to override. (Farrand, 1966, III: 133)

One gets a sense from this excerpt of the more creative capacity of the qualified negative, as compared to the absolute negative, including the mention of the possible involvement of the judiciary in the revision process.

### *The antifederalists*

The views expressed to explain and defend the newly constructed Constitution to the country were summarized in the Federalist Papers.

Needless to say, however, many took issue with the new Constitution and the veto power. These arguments were summarized in the Anti-Federalist Papers. In point of fact, most antifederalists accepted the veto power as a way of "securing executive independence" (Storing, 1981, I: 61); this acceptance was a further indication of the widespread sense that the president needed the veto power to defend himself from congressional aggrandizement.

Complaints about the veto power did arise, nevertheless. One participant in the federal convention who refused to sign the document, Luther Martin, registered reservations about the veto in an address to the Maryland General Assembly. In particular, he took issue with the antimajoritarian aspects of the veto, insofar as a voting bloc of one-third plus one in either house supportive of the president could uphold any veto, thereby depriving the congressional voting majority "of even the faintest shadow of liberty" (Storing, 1981, II: 31). The British monarchical antecedents of this power also raised doubts. "[W]e were eternally troubled with arguments and precedents from the British government" (Storing, 1981, II: 54; V: 195).

Antifederalist Philadelphiensis (this and many other antifederalists used pseudonyms) was relatively sanguine about the veto power. His reasons bear repeating:

> Among the substantial objections to the great powers of the president, that of his *negative* upon the laws, is one of the most inconsiderable, indeed it is more a sound than any thing else; For, if he be a bold enterprising fellow, there is little fear of his ever having to exercise it. . . . [I]f, however, I say, he should not be a man of an enterprising spirit, in that case he will be a *minion* of the aristocratics, doing according to their will and pleasure, and confirming every law they may think proper to make. (Storing, 1981, III: 129)

This prediction of how the veto would be used in future presidencies comes closer to approximating the actual course of events than did most estimates appearing during this time.

An antifederalist writing under the name William Penn raised the separation of powers question, pointing out that six state constitutions contained language which specified that the three branches of government should be "forever separate and distinct from each other"

(Storing, 1981, III: 173). As a legislative power given to the executive, the veto was seen as contradicting the maxim, derived from Montesquieu, that the best way to avoid the abuse of power is to divide it. Penn also noted that even the British king restrained his use of the veto, being sensitive to such intrusion into the legislative realm (Storing, 1981, III: 173–74).

The Albany (New York) Antifederal Committee took the veto power as symptomatic of the president's vast executive powers, which were perceived as superior to those of many European monarchs. Here again, the veto was seen as a power that even kings were reluctant to use (Storing, 1981, VI: 124). Finally, the Impartial Examiner took strong exception to the veto, both as a misapplication of a power from the British system, and as a power liable to upset the political balance. Reflecting on the origins of the veto, the Examiner implored, "let this collateral jurisdiction, which constitutes the *royal negative,* be held by kings alone, since with kings it first originated" (Storing, 1981, V: 196). And on the topic of the danger to political balance posed by the veto, the Examiner speculated that the veto would be rarely overridden in practice. Thus armed with such a power, the president "cannot be the object of any laws; he will be above all law: as none can be enacted without his consent—he will be elevated to the height of supremacy" (Storing, 1981, V: 196).

## Conclusion

Since its first chronicled use, the veto has been inextricably connected with the lawmaking process, especially as the crucial connecting link between the executive and the legislalure. For obvious reasons, the British experience provides the most pertinent history for the American veto. Like a whittled down stick, the veto was finally all that was left of the British monarchs' once-supreme lawmaking authority. Yet even when the king's only recourse was the veto, the power served as a useful prod for political bargaining. The veto issue even became intertwined with the issue of legislative riders.

The colonial experience illustrated from the start that a strong executive also meant a strong (in the case of royal colonial governors an absolute) veto. The initial American reaction embodied governing by legislative supremacy and executive subordination: the elimination of veto powers. But the unsatisfactory governing consequences of weak executives led, first in New York and later at the federal convention, to a reinvigorated executive, which meant also the bestowal of the veto power, this time in qualified form. Yet the veto was not viewed as simply a checking or blocking device. It was a revisionary power, seen as part of a larger process and allowing the president to play an active role in improving legislation. The veto was a block, too—against a dominating legislature trying to impinge on the executive and against irredeemably bad legislation—but it was later political squabbling that caused the revisionary aspect to be lost.

In the years following the Constitutional Convention, the veto appeared at the center of numerous political disputes. During the nineteenth century in particular, controversy over the veto power arose in ways that revealed the changing role of the presidency. The founders, however, would have found these controversies surprising.[9]

# 2

# Evolution of the Veto Power

*Naturally the veto power did not escape the early talent of Americans for conjuring up constitutional limitations out of thin air.*

Edward S. Corwin (1957)

As with virtually every power enumerated in the Constitution, the veto power evolved over time as experimentation, circumstance, and cumulative precedent combined to give the power its actual shape, especially as to its frequency, and other conditions of use. The purpose of this chapter is to explore how the parameters and perceptions of the veto power changed, in particular as they relate to the presidency itself. Exercise of the veto power contributed to an expansion of presidential power, particularly over the legislative realm, and this change occurred primarily in noncrisis, domestic circumstances. (In times of crisis, normal powers such as the veto recede in importance as the country [including the Congress] looks to the president for leadership and is willing to accept his greater use of power.) The veto affects the presidency primarily in the domestic arena since the veto power comes into play with Congress and is not a power directly related to the conduct of foreign affairs (aside from the presidential opportunity to veto bills having to do with foreign relations). The president's greater influence over foreign policy (Wildavsky, 1966) infers that vetoes are less likely in this area in any case.

Although use of the veto has expanded the presidency, the delicate politics of that power are demonstrated by the fact that vigorous use of the veto has been politically detrimental to the presidents involved. With two exceptions, every president who relied significantly on the veto (thus defending and often extending the accepted use of the power) suffered politically. They were casualties in the struggle to strengthen and enhance presidential powers, but they succeeded (as the following sections demonstrate) in rolling back the perceived limitations on the veto power.

Admittedly, the constitutional and historical arguments by congressional and other critics who dissented from presidential vetoes were founded, in large part, on partisan differences. Yet, as the nineteenth century wore on, partisanship was, if anything, enhanced. The constitutionally based arguments against instances of veto use receded, and the liberal interpretation of veto use eventually predominated among both presidential friends and foes. (The focus here is this debate over the *nature* of the veto power and the interaction between presidency and Congress. The substance of particular vetoes is sometimes discussed, but the aim is not to describe all vetoes, nor to describe the vetoes of all presidents. For discussions of the vetoes themselves, see Mason [1890] and Jackson [1967].)

The veto has not, by any means, been the sole vehicle for the well-recognized expansion of presidential power. But it is vitally important to understand that presidential expansion has occurred not only in times of crisis and through the actions of forceful leaders (Lincoln, the Roosevelts, Wilson, etc.), but also in times of noncrisis under presidents not generally perceived as dynamic, forceful leaders. In general, these unspectacular presidents are perceived as less successful and/or less important because they lost support, failed to resolve problems, and otherwise seemed to lack adroit leadership skills. Though all of this may be true, the great fallacy is the presumption that since these presidents somehow failed to lead, they therefore contributed little or nothing to the strong modern presidency. Nothing could be further from the truth. As the story of the veto will show, even 'failed' presidencies, such as those of Tyler and Andrew Johnson, helped to advance the accepted bounds of presidential prerogative. This argument—that use of the veto usually hurts presidents but helps the presidency—is not offered with any presumption that a strong or stronger presidency is a good thing; compelling arguments can be made for both strong-presidency and restrained-presidency views. Rather, the argument promotes the straightforward claim that even those presidents who 'fall in battle' contribute, like soldiers on the battlefield, to the presidential 'victory' of a stronger presidency. The presidency has certainly expanded through many avenues, for a variety of reasons. Yet so much attention has been focused on a few crucial decisions by a few 'great' presidents that the importance of more routine, everyday decisionmaking (especially in a historical context) has been pretty much ignored or left to historians of particular presidents or particular eras of history.

### *The first vetoes*

As with so many facets of the presidency, institutional precedent was set by the first chief executive. President Washington was keenly aware of the precedent-setting nature of his actions, and, as the presiding officer at the Constitutional Convention, he had been a party to the debates, including consideration of the veto power.

At the start of his first term, Washington considered withholding his signature from a tonnage bill as an expression of displeasure. Though not a veto, it aroused enough concern that members of the Senate promised to accommodate the president's objections in a subsequent bill in exchange for his signature. A few days after this, Washington indicated in a letter to James Madison (then a member of the House of Representatives) that he was considering a veto of a pay bill for the members of Congress. The bill set equal salaries for members of both chambers, but Washington was of the opinion that senators should receive higher pay. He asked Madison his opinion of such a veto in correspondence marked "Confidential." Madison's response is not known, but Washington signed the bill in question on September 22, 1789. He may have felt the bill too trivial to warrant the first presidential veto, or he may have decided to refrain from interfering with an essentially internal matter of congressional pay (Thomson, 1978: 28).

In February of 1791, Washington seriously considered a veto of the Hamilton-inspired bill to establish a national bank. This major bill was, in the view of many, an unconstitutional intrusion by Congress into fiscal affairs. The president solicited advisory opinions from Attorney General Edmund Randolph, Secretary of State Thomas Jefferson, and Madison, all of whom recommended veto. Washington even asked Madison to draft a possible veto message. Finally, he solicited the opinion of Hamilton, who presented a memo to Washington (on the ninth day after passage of the bill) that made a case for the bank based on the doctrine of implied powers. Hamilton's arguments were so compelling and important that they eventually made their way into Justice Marshall's opinion in the landmark Supreme Court case of *McCulloch v. Maryland* (1819). On the last day of the ten-day period, Washington signed the bill.

The first actual veto occurred on April 5, 1792. The bill in question dealt with congressional reapportionment. The Constitution called for an apportionment in the House based on the ratio of one representative for every thirty thousand people. Yet the bill passed gave more representation than this to some of the larger states in an effort to compensate for the remainder of these states' populations over the thirty thousand multiple (so that the total number of representatives in the House would equal the total population of the country divided by thirty thousand). Jefferson objected strenuously to Washington, as the bill seemed plainly unconstitutional; Jefferson added his concern that, after four years in office, "non-use of his negative begins already to excite a belief that no President will ever venture to use it" (Thomson, 1978: 30). Washington was sympathetic to Jefferson's arguments and on the tenth day after passage, the president met with Jefferson to discuss the bill. The men discussed the bill's primary political problem—that the reapportionment scheme would benefit mostly northern states and that a veto might appear to be a sop to the South—but noted too that it had passed by a bare majority in both houses, indicating that a veto would not likely be overridden. At the conclusion of the meeting, Washington sent for Randolph and Madison who, with Jefferson, drew up a veto message, whereupon it was sent immediately to the House. The underlying rationale for the veto was clearly a constitutional question. The bill was, in Jefferson's words, "contrary to the common understanding of that instrument [the Constitution]" (Watson, 1910: I, 373). Jefferson was also highly pleased that the veto had at last been used: "[I]t gave pleasure to have at length an instance of the negative being exercised" (Thomson, 1978: 30). The House considered a motion to override, but it fell far short of the necessary two-thirds. The Congress soon thereafter passed a substitute bill with a new apportionment scheme; this was passed and signed without problem.

Washington's second and final veto occurred four days before the end of his presidency, and it involved a bill that included a provision to reduce the size of the already small army by disbanding two dragoon companies. Acting essentially on his own this time, Washington argued in his veto message that the dragoons were needed and that the move to disband the companies was unfair to the men involved. This time, the veto justification had nothing to do with the Constitution; it was purely and simply a disagreement over policy. The House failed in its attempt to override the veto. It then proceeded immediately to pass the same bill, this time with the offending provision excised. Washington signed the new bill on March 3, 1797, his last day in office. Interestingly, Washington's second veto had the effect of an item veto insofar as Congress removed the provision in question in response to the veto message identifying the objectionable portion. Ironically, Washington addressed this very issue four years previously, in a letter to Edmund Pendleton, in which he also summarized his philosophy about the veto:

> You do me no more than Justice when you suppose that from motives of respect to the Legislature (and I might add from my interpretation of the Constitution) I give my Signature to many Bills with which my Judgment is at variance. In declaring this, however, I allude to no particular Act. From the nature of the Constitution, I must approve all the parts of a Bill, or reject it in toto. To do the latter can only be Justified upon the clear and obvious ground of propriety; and I never had such confidence in my own faculty of judging as to be over tenacious of the opinions I may have imbibed in doubtful cases. (Zinn, 1951: 22)

Here we see in Washington's assessment of the veto a reflection of his restrained view of the presidency as a whole. He was not inclined to veto any given bill simply because he disagreed with it, in part or whole. Nor did he consider his wisdom and judgment to be inherently above that of Congress. Yet the functional constraints he observes on the veto are not of a constitutional nature but rather those which emphasize his own values of propriety and restraint. Nevertheless, as Washington's second veto shows, he considered the president's policy judgment to be an acceptable rationale for use of the veto.

Already, the first presidential administration had exemplified many of the accepted features of the veto. Its two applications provided cases of both constitutionally and policy-justified vetoes. The legitimacy of the president's mature judgment in deciding whether to veto was accepted. The use of the veto as a positive policy-shaping tool was also demonstrated, and there was even a glint of the item-veto controversy yet to come. Finally, as historian Carlton Jackson (1967: 4) observed: "The real importance of these vetoes was not what they were about or what they said, but simply that they occurred."

Neither of Washington's two successors, John Adams and Thomas Jefferson, applied the veto in their collective twelve years in office.[1] In the case of Adams, this is something of an irony, as he had been a proponent of absolute veto powers for the president (Thomson, 1978: 28). Despite Jefferson's eagerness to have Washington use the veto, he seemed to share the first president's sense of restraint and gravity when it came to actual veto use. Jefferson summarized his view of the veto this way:

> Unless the president's mind on a view of everything which is urged for and against a bill is tolerably clear that it is unauthorized by the Constitution, if the pro and con hang so even as to balance his judgment, a just respect for the wisdom of Legislature would naturally decide in favor of their opinion. It is chiefly for cases where they are clearly misled by error, ambition or interest that the Constitution has placed a check in the negative of the President. (Watson, 1910: I, 373)

The question of constitutionality evidently played a key role in Jefferson's thinking, but so did consideration of "error, ambition or interest" as reflected in congressional enactments.

The first president to use the veto with vigor (and who therefore received national attention for its use) was James Madison. Of the seven bills he vetoed in office, he relied on a Constitutional justification for five. The other two bills, relating to naturalization and bank incorporation, were vetoed on policy grounds. The most controversial veto was that of the bank bill. Yet the controversy was not based on the absence of a constitutional justification for the veto. Madison acknowledged at the start of his veto message that such a proposal was, in his view, constitutional (*Messages,* 1913: I, 540). Rather, the bank issue was simply one of the most controversial questions of the time. Madison was criticized harshly by members of Congress and in various newspapers around the country in what was part of a vigorous national debate over the precarious economic situation of the country (Jackson, 1967: 9–10). Yet for all the controversy and criticism surrounding this veto, it was sustained, as were all of Madison's vetoes.

Madison was also the first president to employ the pocket veto. The first of two occurred in July, 1812. When Congress reconvened in November, Madison worked with Congress to iron out the disputed provisions, and the revised bill was then passed and signed (Jackson, 1967: 8–9). Madison's second pocket veto occurred in 1816 and aroused little attention.

Despite Madison's more vigorous use of the veto, he was still working within the veto logic established by Washington. Similarly, Madison's critics also limited debate to the issues at hand and were not questioning the constitutional basis of the manner in which the veto was being employed.

Madison's successor, James Monroe, employed the veto but once, in 1822. He had laid the groundwork for that one veto in his first annual message to the Congress, delivered on December 2, 1817. The matter in question involved an issue raised by Madison—the constitutional right of the Congress to establish and finance internal improvements, primarily roads and canals. In his message, Monroe sought to inform Congress clearly from the outset as to his views on the matter: "[I]t would be improper after what has passed that this discussion should be revived with an uncertainty of my opinion respecting the right. Disregarding early impressions I have bestowed on the subject . . . the result is a settled conviction in my mind that Congress do not possess the right. It is not contained in any of the specified powers granted to Congress, nor can I consider it incidental to or a necessary means . . . for carrying into effect any of the powers which are specifically granted" (*Messages,* 1913: I, 587).

Monroe went on to suggest passage of a constitutional amendment to grant Congress the right to undertake such internal improvement projects. In his 1822 veto message, Monroe reiterated these arguments in a brief veto message. He appended to that message, however, an extremely lengthy, detailed document summarizing his views on the subject of internal improvements (*Messages,* 1913: I, 711–52; his veto was upheld).

In the aftermath of Monroe's clear threat to use the veto, stated in his 1817 message, a House committee was set up, chaired by Henry Tucker of Virginia, to review the portion of the message relating to Monroe's views on public works. In their report, issued

December 15, 1817, they stated their view that the president's expression of opinion should have no influence over congressional actions whatsoever. They further proposed that, should a presidential statement announcing a possible veto be made and have the effect of deterring Congress from enacting a measure they might otherwise pass, "the Presidential veto would acquire a force unknown to the Constitution, and the legislative body would be shorn of its powers from a want of confidence in its strength" (*Annals of Congress,* December 15, 1817: 452). The fear that a veto threat would retard congressional lawmaking never materialized in the dire form predicted. The use of the veto threat has, admittedly, become an important ancillary power of the veto; it has not, however, transformed the veto into a dictatorial device. Ironically, within thirty years, members of Congress would be criticizing presidential vetoes when they occurred *without* prior warning from the president.

An even more interesting irony about the veto threat is that it was understood by the founding fathers to be an acceptable and even useful component of the veto itself. Hamilton (*Federalist Papers,* #73, 1961: 446) wrote of the veto's "silent and unperceived, though forcible, operation. When men, engaged in unjustifiable pursuits, are aware that obstructions may come from a quarter which they cannot control, they will often be restrained by the bare apprehension of opposition from doing what they would with eagerness rush into if no such external impediments were to be feared."

Four months after the committee report, Virginia Congressman William J. Lewis introduced a series of five related constitutional amendments. The first called for the president to be stripped of his approval/disapproval power over legislation, which effectively meant loss of the veto. The other four proposals gave Congress sole power of appointment and removal of executive and judicial officials (*House Journal,* April 16, 1818: 478–79). Whether the proposed amendments were provoked by the prior committee report is not known; but Congressmen Tucker and Lewis were both Virginia Democrats. This was the first recorded instance of an attempt to strip the president of his veto powers. It would certainly not be the last.

Monroe's successor, John Quincy Adams, exercised no vetoes. He shared the opinion of his predecessors that the veto should be "exercised with great reserve" (Pessen, 1975: 135). After his presidency, Adams served many years as a member of the House, where he played an active role in many veto controversies.

## The Jacksonian veto

Andrew Jackson's presidency marked an important turning point for the veto and for the presidency itself. Jackson vetoed more bills (twelve) than all of his six predecessors combined. Despite the greater number, the form of these vetoes was not unique. Of the twelve, seven were pocket vetoes; yet Madison had used the pocket veto twice. Seven of the bills involved public works; yet Jackson not only based these on constitutional grounds but relied on the logic and precedent of similar Madison and Monroe vetoes. Jackson's most controversial veto, involving the bank bill, also followed in the footsteps of a bank bill veto by Madison.

Several factors did, however, separate Jackson from his predecessors. He had announced prior to his first two vetoes that he would in fact veto these public works bills, should they cross his desk. By way of explanation, Jackson felt, as had his predecessors, that public works were necessary and important but that Congress did not have the constitutional authority to enact many of the projects it promoted. When Monroe had announced his reservations about a bill before it reached his desk, the action prompted outcry. When Jackson did the same, it had a similar but more forceful consequence. Viewing such a statement as a kind of prior restraint on the legislature, many of its members reacted with outrage, arguing that such statements were an improper, even unconstitutional attempt by the president to regulate the legislative process by discouraging action that might otherwise result in legislation (Jackson, 1967: 16–17). Nevertheless, Jackson was to do this often, usually through his annual messages to Congress.

A word about Jackson's veto philosophy is in order. Despite his more frequent use of the veto, his views about its gravity were consonant with those of the times. In his 1830 annual message (*Messages,* 1913: II, 1075), he expressed the "reluctance and anxiety" that he felt whenever he considered using the veto, especially when it dealt with other than constitutional issues. He also said that the veto "should not be exercised on slight occasions" and only "in matters of deep interest." But even if these sentiments were not completely sincere, they indicate at least the preeminence of the view of the time that the veto should be used sparingly, with great care and circumspection. After offering these comments, however, Jackson departed from tradition by saying that, if he was mistakenly representing the views of the people, they could simply turn him out of office. Thus, he would stick to his course and let the people judge the consequences at reelection time. Here, surely, was the embodiment of Jacksonian democracy. As Corwin (1957: 21) observed, "Jackson became the first President in our history to appeal to the people over the heads of their legislative representatives." Jackson's populist posture infuriated congressional critics. As John C. Calhoun, for example, raged, "He claims to be not only the representative, but the immediate representative of the American people! What effrontery! What boldness of assertion! The Immediate representative? Why, he never received a vote from the American people. He was elected by the electors—the colleges" (Ford, 1967: 180).

Although all twelve of Jackson's vetoes contained constitutional justifications, the logic of the public works vetoes was considered inconsistent, as Jackson vetoed some, but encouraged other legislation of a like nature (Jackson, 1967: 18–19). This perceived inconsistency emerged with greatest force with his 1832 veto of the bank bill, referred to by one historian as "the most celebrated veto in American history" (Jackson, 1967: 29). Skowronek (1984: 94) referred to Jackson's bank veto message as "a regime-builder's manifesto." In it Jackson argued that some of the powers granted to the national bank were unconstitutional. While acknowledging that the Supreme Court had previously ruled favorably on the bank, such precedent need not, even ought not to be the criterion for the president's judgment on the issue. Each branch of government was entitled to judge for itself the constitutionality of important issues. Simply because the court had ruled the bank constitutional did not perforce mean that the president could not veto the bill, on constitutional or other grounds, if he felt the necessity to do so (*Messages,* 1913: II, 1139–54). Thus, supplementing the constitutional rationale was a loudly broadcast subtext—that the president need only rely on his political judgment in making a veto decision. Though this conclusion was not inconsistent with the intent of the framers, nor even with the vetoes of some of Jackson's predecessors, it was a view that had never been so broadly and baldly articulated by a sitting president. It was this overtly independent attitude that prompted one commentator (Ford, 1967: 179–80) to observe in 1898 that the veto under Jackson "developed a terrible power. His twelve vetoes descended upon Congress like the blows of an iron flail."

Jackson's veto message provoked a storm of debate. Transcripts of the debate consumed seventy-five pages in the *Debates in Congress.* The most long-winded speaker was, not surprisingly, Daniel Webster. In a speech highly critical of Jackson's veto, Webster labored to illustrate the inconsistencies and faults in the veto message. As with many of Jackson's critics, Webster alluded to the seemingly monarchical nature of Jackson's views toward legislation and the veto. "According to the doctrines put forth by the President, although Congress may have passed a law, and although the Supreme Court may have pronounced it constitutional, yet it is, nevertheless, no law at all, if he, in his good pleasure, sees fit to deny its effect, in other words, to repeal and annul it" (*Debates,* July 11, 1832: 1232). This use of the veto was, in Webster's view, as bad as the worst excesses during the Tudor and Stuart eras in England.

Unlike some critics, Webster's discontent was not founded in the underlying motive of expedience in Jackson's veto, but rather primarily on Jackson's expansive definition of his own prerogatives. Webster shrewdly observed that "if . . . the President sees fit to negative a bill, on the ground of its being inexpedient or impolitic, he has a right to do so" (*Debates,* July 11, 1832: 1234). Webster did take strong issue, however, with Jackson's presumption that he should have been consulted in the framing of the bill as a means to avoid a veto: "[T]he [veto] message proceeds to claim for the President, not the power of approval, but the primary power, the power of originating laws" (*Debates,* July 11, 1832: 1239–40).

The notion of presidential involvement in legislative drafting and modification, so much taken for granted today, was almost revolutionary during this time; yet, it flowed directly from the logic of the veto power. If a veto was to be avoided as a strong action against legislation, an obvious way to do so would be to take the president's wishes into account while the bill was in its formative stages. Jackson shocked many be asserting this boldly. Even in the absence of Jackson's actions, however, greater involvement of the president in the legislative process was inevitable given the presence and at least occasional use of the veto power.

Senator Clayton echoed objections similar to Webster's. Referring back to Jackson's annual messages of 1829 and 1830, Clayton mocked Jackson's request for prior involvement by saying that "Congress is lectured because it did not submit the matter to the Executive before it dared to act" (*Debates,* July 11, 1832: 1261). In his speech against the veto, Henry Clay fell back on an argument more frequently cited, though more suspect by today's standards. He argued that the veto was considered by the founders to be "an extraordinary power . . . not . . . to be used in ordinary cases." Surely, though, the bank veto was no ordinary case. Clay went on to state incorrectly that Madison had used the veto only two or three times (Madison vetoed seven bills) and to argue that Jackson's apparently more frequent use contradicted the intent of the founders. Clay then asserted his broader objection to the veto power: that it was "hardly reconcilable with the genius of representative Government," especially "if it is to be frequently employed to the expediency of measures." It was a power that even kings had abandoned. Clay also questioned whether the founders would have condoned a veto involving an issue so long debated: "It cannot be imagined that the convention contemplated the application of the veto to a question which has been so long, so often, and so thoroughly scrutinized, as that of the Bank of the United States" (*Debates,* July 12, 1832: 1265–66). This argument is, to say the least, innovative.

Clay condemned, too, and at some length, the president's request for prior consultation, as he found it to be "totally new in the practice, and utterly contrary to the theory of the Government." He also questioned the validity of Jackson's consideration of the motives and degree of support for the bill in the Congress as pertinent to the veto justification (*Debates,* July 12, 1832: 1272).

Jackson's principal defender in the Senate was Senator Benton. On the final day of discussion (July 13), Benton defended Jackson and criticized the national bank. In the process, he also engaged in rancorous words with Clay. The override motion was finally put to a vote, and the veto was sustained, 22–19.

Jackson's bald statement of executive power combined with another aspect of Jackson's veto use that surfaced initially in his December 6, 1830 annual message. The previous May, Jackson had pocket vetoed two public works bills after Congress had adjourned *sine die* (literally, "without a day," as when Congress adjourns without setting a day for reconvening). The bills were not, however, given an absolute veto, as Jackson told the Congress six months later that "I was compelled to retain them" because, as he said, he had not had sufficient time to consider the bills properly at the rushed end of the session ending in May. He then returned them to Congress in December (*Messages,* 1913: II, 1071). This unprecedented retention of bills resembled, to his critics, the manner in which British kings had exercised their veto powers, giving rise to the criticism that Jackson was attempting to establish a de facto monarchy (Jackson, 1967: 24–27). Jackson's archenemy, Henry Clay, observed after a similar retention in 1833 that the president's action was "arbitrary and unconstitutional" (*Debates,* December 5, 1833: 18).[2] This retention of bills appeared in no other presidency, and was clearly swept aside in a twentieth century Supreme Court case.[3]

One final factor adding to the Jacksonian stew pot was the changing nature of the country. As the nation grew, so too did sectional and partisan splits. The consequently sharper differences evidenced themselves in Washington and did much to fan the disputes centering on Jackson's policies and approach to governing. Such issues as the bank and internal improvements, the principal subjects of Jacksonian vetoes, engendered strong sectional feelings.

Jackson's aggressive use of the veto and his attendant controversial approach to governing prompted the Senate to consider and approve a motion to censure the president on March 28, 1834. During debate, Clay claimed that Jackson had made an "assertion of a power which was greater than that possessed by any king in Europe," and that he (Jackson) "wished to ascend the throne" (*Congressional Globe,* March 27, 1834: 269–70). Clay had considered a move to impeach but cast it aside as nearly impossible, since, according to him, any marshall or civil officer designated to serve a summons on the president could be simply dismissed by the president, and Jackson had control not only of governmental officers but of the army and navy as well. Yet, Clay said, it was "the right and duty of the Senate to express an opinion, and the resolution [to censure] was nothing more" (*Congressional Globe,* March 27, 1834: 269). It is also likely that Clay would never have succeeded in getting articles of impeachment passed through the House (where impeachment proceedings must begin), as it was more strongly allied with Jackson. The motion to censure passed the Senate by a vote of 26–20.[4]

On April 15, Jackson issued a lengthy response to the Senate. In it, he said that the Senate's resolution was "wholly unauthorized by the Constitution, and in derogation of its entire spirit" (*Messages,* 1913: II, 1291). Jackson included in his rebuttal to the Senate the texts of resolutions from the state legislatures of Maine, New Jersey, and Ohio, all of which affirmed their support for Jackson's vetoes as being both wise and constitutional. Jackson also pointed out that four senators from these three states voted for his censure, clearly contrary to the sentiments of the bodies that elected them (*Messages,* 1913: II, 1306–9).

Three times during Jackson's presidency (1833, 1835 and 1836), members of Congress introduced constitutional amendments to change the veto override to a simple majority. Senator Joseph Kent offered such a motion on February 20, 1835.[5] In his floor comments, he observed that the veto power unites executive and legislative powers, and such a combination in the hands of the president leads to despotism and oppression. He then observed that the veto was designed "only to prevent legislative encroachment upon the executive authority" and only for bills raising constitutional problems. Kent also noted Jefferson's contrasting nonuse of the veto in his eight-year presidency and cited other sources to argue that the veto should be used sparingly and with caution, while Jackson had used it "till it has become an occurrence of almost every day." Kent concluded by citing the far greater tendency of executives, as opposed to legislatures, to aggrandize power (*Congressional Globe,* February 20, 1835: 269–70). After Jackson's presidency, at least nine similar constitutional amendments were proposed in the nineteenth century (in 1838, twice in 1841, three times in 1842, and once in 1849, 1850, and 1884).

Despite the sentiments of Jackson's opponents, many people supported his actions. Indeed, Jackson's reelection was widely seen as a referendum on his 1832 bank bill veto. Writing at about this time, Supreme Court Justice Joseph Story (1833: 350–51), appointed to the court by Madison, retained a positive view of the existing veto power, citing its several benefits. Story wrote about the veto during the height of the Jackson veto storm that "the real danger is, that the executive will use the power too rarely." In his view, "Nothing but a gross abuse of the power upon frivolous, or party pretenses, to secure a petty triumph, or to defeat a wholesome restraint, would bring it [the veto] into contempt, or odium." There was no indication in his writings that Story thought Jackson had abused the veto powers, though by the standards of the time, many felt that Jackson had indeed committed such "gross abuse." Nevertheless, he retained his popularity, served out the remainder of his second term, and set a precedent for veto use that would forever change the presidency.

## Harrison and the Tyler crisis

The veto controversy lay dormant throughout the term of Jackson's handpicked successor, Martin Van Buren, who applied the veto only once, in the form of a pocket veto. The nation's first full-scale economic depression did much to bring an end to the Jackson–Van Buren era, allowing for the election of Whig William Henry Harrison in 1840. The Whig antipathy to Jackson's executive style found full expression in Harrison, as seen, for example, in his pledge to serve only a single term in office. In President Harrison's inaugural address (the longest ever given), he outlined the features of a Whiggish presidency. The centrality of the veto to executive power is seen in the fact that one-eighth of his text was devoted solely to discussion of the veto. He summarized his view of the veto by saying: "I consider the veto power . . . solely as a conservative power, to be used only, first, to protection the Constitution from violation; secondly, the people from the effects of hasty legislation where their will has been probably disregarded or not well understood, and, thirdly, to prevent the effects of combinations violative of the rights of minorities" (*Messages,* 1913: III, 1866).

Harrison thought it "preposterous" that the president would presume to have a keener sense of popular sentiment than members of Congress. In observing the apparently antimajoritarian nature of the veto, he rationalized its inclusion in the Constitution as explainable only on the assumption that the founders could not have intended it to be of "any benefit to the ordinary course of legislation." Moreover, Harrison was unequivocal in rejecting Jackson's approach. "To assist or control Congress, then, in its ordinary legislation could not, I conceive, have been the motive for conferring the veto power on the President. This argument acquires additional force from the fact of its never having been thus used by the first six Presidents" (*Messages,* 1913: III, 1864–65). Harrison was incorrect in his latter assertion.

Still, his speech evidences the tendency to seek justification for views on the veto from past practice and the founders' intent. The problem with this is twofold: First, it elevates tradition above, and excludes contemporary circumstances; second, actual past practices were (and continue to be) distorted, either by design or ignorance, to support a current political view. These problems have not been limited to the veto debate, but are clearly exemplified by it.

Harrison's most lengthy inaugural was followed by the nation's briefest presidency. With Harrison's death, Whig Vice President John Tyler was elevated to the presidency. As the first vice president to become president by succession, a certain degree of ambivalence surrounded his time in office. Members of Congress and others could not decide whether he should exercise full presidential powers or act merely as a caretaker. Nor could they decide at first what to call him. The House passed a resolution referring to him as president. In the Senate, a resolution recommending that he be called vice president was defeated (Chitwood, 1964: 206). Many resented and disliked 'His Accidency' Tyler from the start, including House member John Quincy Adams and Henry Clay, who, though a Whig supportive of Tyler at the start, had been deprived the presidential nod in 1840. From the start, however, Tyler assumed for himself full presidential powers and duties, setting an important precedent for future vice presidents.

The bank issue continued to be a preeminent political concern, and, with a Whig in the White House, most assumed that passage was assured. Yet on August 16, 1841, Tyler vetoed the bank bill, citing constitutional reasons relating to states' rights and his own consistent opposition to such a proposal. Though there had been some indications of his opposition to a national bank earlier in his career, Tyler had mostly kept his views to himself and gave no hint that a veto was impending before it occurred (Chitwood, 1964: 225). In fact, in his inaugural address of April 9, Tyler said: "I shall promptly give my sanction to any constitutional measure which . . . shall have for its object the restoration of a sound circulating medium" (*Messages,* 1913: III, 1892).

In the veto's aftermath, the president was congratulated by Democrats (one veteran Democrat observed of Tyler, "Egad, he has found one of old Jackson's pens and it wouldn't write anyway but plain and straightforward" (Chitwood, 1964: 231), scorned by Whigs, and was subjected to unprecedented public signs of disapproval. For example, when the veto message was read in the Senate, some spectators in the gallery hissed. Senator Benton protested until an arrest was made and apologies extended (*Congressional Globe,* August 16, 1841: 338–39). That night, a "mob" of about thirty gathered in front of the White House after midnight, making a loud disturbance that unsettled the occupants. The following night, a figure of Tyler was burned in effigy near the presidential residence (Chitwood, 1964: 228–29).

In the Senate, bank supporters sought to delay reconsideration of the vetoed bill in the vain hope of winning enough support to clinch an override. But finally, debate and a vote were held on August 19. Henry Clay led the attack on Tyler. In his speech, he maintained a veneer of respect in his discussion of the veto but suggested also that Tyler could have registered his reservations by letting the bill become law without his signature, or that he might even resign from the presidency, both as protest, and because (in Clay's view) Tyler's views ran counter to the majority of the country. Senator Rives of Virginia (Tyler's home state) defended the president, arguing that he was merely upholding his oath of office, properly exercising his powers against an unconstitutional proposal. Rives also refuted Clay's inference that majority support for a measure in Congress impelled the president to give his assent in deference to popular will (*Congressional Globe,* August 19, 1841: app., 364–70). The Senate voted to uphold the veto, 25–24. The next day, members of the Senate briefly debated the nature of the veto power. This debate would escalate in subsequent months.

After the veto, an effort was made to accommodate the views of the president in a new bank bill. Whigs sent a representative, Congressman Stuart of Virginia, to see the president, who gave his approval to a compromise plan. After cautioning Stuart to avoid exposing him to charges of directing congressional affairs, Tyler grasped Stuart's hand and exclaimed, "Stuart! if you can be instrumental in passing this bill through Congress, I will esteem you the best friend I have on earth" (Chitwood, 1964: 239). Two days later, Tyler told his cabinet that a new bank bill could be ready within two days. Congress obliged him; yet on September 9, he again vetoed the bill. Tyler paid dearly for his politically maladroit actions.

In his second veto message, Tyler adopted conciliatory language (he rendered the veto "with extreme regret") and attempted to explain his philosophy concerning the veto. He considered the veto to be a device inserted by the framers "as a great, conservative principle," to be "most cautiously exerted, and perhaps never except in a case eminently involving the public interest." If the president abides by his "mental and moral" convictions he must use the veto when circumstance dictates; to not do so would be to "commit an act of gross moral turpitude." Tyler also rejected out of hand the notion that majority support for a bill in Congress should constrain the use of the veto (*Messages,* 1913: III, 1921–22).

Tyler's statement of veto principles was on generally firm ground, especially given the temper of the times. But his vacillation on the bank issue, especially after the first veto, infuriated members of Congress and much of the country. In response to the veto, Tyler's entire cabinet resigned, with the exception of Secretary of State Daniel Webster. Tyler's elucidation of his views on the veto seemed, if anything, to further inflame the opposition. On September 10, Congressman John Minor Botts took the floor after an unsuccessful attempt to interrupt House consideration of the veto by considering first a constitutional amendment to lower the veto override to a simple majority. Botts spared little in his vituperation against Tyler, charging him with, among other things, "perfidy and treachery." He also reminded the chamber of Tyler's prior condemnation of Jackson's vetoes. Congressman Jones questioned the nature of the debate, as it sounded like a discussion of impeachment charges, while the business at hand was simply a veto override.

Congressman Mason delivered a lengthy address (later reprinted by the *National Intelligencer*) about the veto. He questioned out loud how he might explain to his constituents that Congress's laborious work on the bank bill was abruptly frustrated by an unexpected veto. He then went on to refer, as did many others, to the monarchical roots of the veto power:

> Is it not calculated to excite astonishment that one of the cast-off, disgraced, and obsolete prerogatives of the Crown of Great Britain should have been dug up from a dishonored grave, to which the indignant voice of that nation had consigned it, and borne across the Atlantic, to be transplanted in the soil of republican America—here to be nourished and defended as 'the tree of life' in our garden of Eden? (Mason, 1841: 6)

To Mason, the veto was "his royal prerogative." It was, moreover, effectively an absolute veto, since no veto had been overridden up to this time, in part because the president's patronage was sufficient to win at least one-third support in one house. The veto could only be justified, said Mason, for presidential self-defense against legislative encroachments. "Applied to any other purpose, it becomes an engine of the most odious tyranny." As employed by Tyler, the veto was being used beyond appropriate bounds; to Mason, there was no difference between usurpation of power and abuse of power. The veto had become "the great disturbing 'principle of our system' " (Mason, 1841: 8).

In his assertion of severe limits on the veto power, Mason committed a common fallacy. He cited Hamilton's arguments for the veto in Federalist #73, which defended the veto as necessary for executive defense, for use against bad laws, and as a power which would be used rarely. Yet Mason argued that these conditions posed the *only* circumstances under which the veto could be used, when in fact Hamilton was plainly stating instead, for the first two conditions, why the veto was necessary. Hamilton's third point of rare use was both a prediction and a reassurance that the veto would probably not be used often. In no sense were these conditions articulated as limitations on the circumstances of veto use (though Tyler had conformed to all three). When the House finally voted, it upheld the veto 103–71.

As Mason's harangue against the veto illustrated, Tyler's two vetoes rubbed a nerve still tender from the Jacksonian period. The following January 24, Henry Clay again introduced a constitutional amendment to reduce the veto override to a simple majority. Clay recited the now-familiar arguments that the veto was undemocratic and monarchical. He also argued that the veto allowed the president to improperly intrude himself into the lawmaking process, and that generally "there had been a constant encroaching by the Executive on the Legislative authority" (*Congressional Globe,* January 24, 1842: 165). Clay emphasized that the failure of any override attempt made it effectively an absolute veto. Senator Preston responded to Clay by arguing that the veto had been considered indispensable by the founders, and that its current use simply represented changing views about policy, therefore not warranting a change as drastic as amending the Constitution.

From February through August of 1842, the Senate and House engaged in periodic, lengthy discourses on the veto power. The transcripts of these speeches and debates consume hundreds of pages in the *Congressional Globe.* This debate was prolonged by two more controversial vetoes in June and August of the same year.

One of the most thoughtful and thorough speeches on the veto power was delivered by Senator (later President) James Buchanan, in response to one of Senator Clay's many attempts to amend the veto power. Buchanan labored to demonstrate that the veto was not monarchical in design or consequence, as it was "a mere appeal by the President of the people's choice from the decision of Congress to the people themselves" (*Congressional Globe,* February 2, 1842: app., 134). Buchanan shrewdly recognized the political costs suffered by a president who used the veto unwisely or too often, and noted, too, how rarely the veto had been used, given the (by his estimate) over six thousand bills passed by Congress in its first fifty years. Buchanan undercut critics who decried the use of the veto based on expediency by citing Washington's oft-forgotten (or overlooked) second veto of a military bill as an obvious example of a president simply disagreeing with the judgment of Congress. Buchanan emphasized, too, that the president had every right to claim to represent the popular will—a right that Congress often claimed for itself alone, or at least above that of the president. At the same time, the veto could be vital to the protection of minority interests (though Buchanan chose, as an example of such interests, the case of protecting slavery). Buchanan concluded that, of all executive powers, the veto was to be feared least: "It cannot create; it can originate no measure; it can change no existing law; it can destroy no existing institution. It is a mere power to arrest hasty and inconsiderate changes, until the voice of the people, who are alike the masters of Senators, Representatives and President, shall be heard" (*Congressional Globe,* February 2, 1842: app., 141).

Senator Archer took the floor to argue that the veto power had grown from being merely a check to "an engine, formidable to the independent action of the Legislature" (*Congressional Globe,* February, 1842: app., 153–4). Archer's concern that the veto had already become the means for the executive to exert greater influence over the legislative process was, at the least, a correct description of these events. He noted, too, that powers possess their own inertia, and that "it did not require a *dangerous man in the presidency,* to present for exhibition the spectacle of legislation crushed, or shaped by the influence of the power of the veto in the government" (*Congressional Globe,* February, 1842: app., 155).

Senator Woodbury raised in particular two key points. First, he argued that, in fact, the Constitution gives the president not only the right, but the obligation to express his opinion on important issues. Though several provisions in the Constitution actually support this contention, it does not otherwise appear in these debates. Second, Woodbury offered a concise and telling judgment about those who raised constitutional objections to Tyler's vetoes. "It is not vetoes—but vetoes on darling measures—vetoes on Distribution, Internal Improvements, and Banks—all connected with the absorbing strides of the moneyed power, which have excited so much hostility and condemnation" (*Congressional Globe,* February 23, 1842: app., 159).

Reputedly the most ringing oration given on the subject was that of John C. Calhoun (*Congressional Globe,* February 28, 1842: app., 164–68). He argued that the veto was, in Madisonian terms, an important check on the tyranny of the majority. It was a great presidential shield, not a sword. As the founders had said, the veto was necessary to retard the demonstrably more dangerous legislature. At the conclusion of his speech, Calhoun was heartily congratulated by senators from both parties. His eloquence took much of the wind out of Clay's sails.

Several other speakers emphasized what became the most frequently mentioned argument against the veto—that its vigorous use represented an intrusion by the president into the legislative process, when in fact article I, section 1 of the Constitution vested all legislative powers in the Congress. Though not supported by contemporary assessments of the veto power and the intent of the framers, this argument has persisted into modern times. We also begin to see a growing impatience with Tyler's actions, evidenced in a war of words that escalated throughout the summer. As one historian observed, the Twenty-seventh Congress "was perhaps the most bitter assembly in American history" (Jackson, 1967: 75). That bitterness culminated in an impeachment vote.

On June 29, Tyler issued his third veto, this time of a provisional tariff bill. Unlike his first two vetoes, Tyler justified this veto on his substantive objections to the bill itself. Though the veto was expected by members of Congress, it set off a howl of protest and a flood of debate. One Whig newspaper, for example, called Tyler a "corrupt fool and knave who pretends to act as President of the United States," who "ought to be shot down in his tracks, as he walks along" (Jackson, 1967: 66). Debate in Congress was only slightly less scathing. Democratic Congressman Weller pointed an accusing finger at the Whig party for selecting Tyler in the first place to run for vice president, blaming them for nominating him solely because he was from Virginia and for running an issue-less campaign in 1840 (*Congressional Globe,* June 30, 1842: app., 554).[6]

Congressman Stuart challenged the merits of Tyler's arguments, based as they were entirely on the wisdom of the bill. Most arguments, however, centered on the role of the president in legislation, vis-à-vis the veto. Congressman Briggs questioned whether the founders could have possibly intended the veto to be used in the ordinary legislative process. Congressman Tillinghast went even further: "To bring the serious power of the qualified negative into habitual use on all occasions of mere difference of opinion as to expediency, in ordinary legislation on matters of business, is a sort of desecration of its true nature and purpose (*Congressional Globe,* June 30, 1842: app., 888). Congressman Howard challenged Tyler's defenders who said that the president had a proper "co-ordinate legislative power." He found it "perfectly clear," in fact, that this power "is not only unsupported, but absolutely forbidden and precluded by the very language of the Constitution" (*Congressional Globe,* July 2, 1842: app., 808).

Congressman Caruthers conceded that the president could, in fact, veto a bill on constitutional or expediency grounds: "He has the naked physical power to obstruct and defeat the most wholesome and necessary acts Congress can pass" (*Congressional Globe,* July 1, 1842: app., 743). But he rankled at the presumption that the Congress must adapt its bills to the president's wishes or face a veto. This use was a form of presidential dictation which made the "one-man power" intolerable and contrary to the spirit of the Constitution. Congressman Barnard complained that if the president could use the veto to block revenue bills, "then he may dictate—in effect originate—any kind of revenue measure he pleases; and he may compel Congress to come to his terms, or stop the wheels of Government" (*Congressional Globe,* July 1, 1842: app., 769). This line of argument reached its logical (not to say absurd) extreme when Congressman Cooper concluded the

the veto "was intended to prevent the enactment of bad and oppressive laws, not of necessary and good ones" (*Congressional Globe,* July 4, 1842: app., 802).

Present, too, in this debate was invective rarely heard in Congress. Congressman Summers referred to Tyler's veto message as an "ill-tempered, undignified tirade." Congressman Barnard seemed almost to be leveling a charge of insanity at the president when he queried: "Under what strange delusion is the President acting? Who had abused his mind, and brought him to such an act of fatuity and desperation?" Congressman Cooper was even more imaginative, called President Tyler a "stupid yet perfidious devil amongst those cast out of heaven," "a lewd spirit," and "a shrewd devil." Dissatisfied with even this, Cooper compared Tyler to "Judas Iscariot, who sold his Master for thirty pieces of silver. He was both a traitor and an ingrate. Thus the parallel between him and the President starts fair; but to assert that it continues throughout, would be doing injustice to the memory of Judas, who repented, returned the money, and hung himself" (*Congressional Globe,* July 1, August 4, 1842: app., 867, 769, 803). These invectives are repeated at length to dramatize the depth of antipathy engendered by Tyler's three vetoes and the extent to which the period of 'good feeling' after the death of Harrison had worn off. During this debate, too, was the first mention of presidential impeachment.

To be sure, Tyler had defenders, including several congressmen who began their speeches by noting their disinclination to take the floor otherwise. Primarily, his defenders were now starting to make the case that, as Congressman Payne said, "the Constitution gave him [the president] power to do it [veto]. . . . not on constitutional grounds—not on the ground of expediency—but simply on the ground of non-approval" (*Congressional Globe,* July 2, 1842: 714). Congressman Rhett concurred that "the sole criterion of the President's conduct is—approval or disapproval. There is no distinction made as to the character of the bills" (*Congressional Globe,* July 1, 1842: app., 606). If the people are dissatisfied, they can turn the president out.

Despite (or perhaps, because of) the strident rhetoric, Tyler carried the day. On July 4, the override vote was called. The veto was upheld, 114–97.

A month later, Tyler issued his fourth veto of a permanent tariff bill, passed after the failure of the last vetoed bill. If Tyler was consciously seeking a way to whip his opponents into a fury, he could have hardly picked a more effective means. Tyler must have known that this fourth veto would infuriate Congress, given the near-obsequious tone of his veto message. He returned the bill "with unfeigned regret. . . . Nothing can be more painful to any individual called upon to perform the Chief Executive duties under our limited Constitution than to be constrained to withhold his assent from an important measure adopted by the Legislature" (*Messages,* 1913: III, 2036–37).

The public outcry was substantial. "ANOTHER VETO" and "VETO THE FOURTH" were prominent headlines in Whig newspapers. Tyler was called a "rogue and royalist" by the *Jonesborough Whig.* The *Alabama Journal* summarized an article from the *London Times,* which reported that Europeans were aghast at the way the veto power was being used to thwart public will. Even the normally staid *National Intelligencer* accused the president of "arrogating powers" over the legislature (Jackson, 1967: 70).

After return of the bill to the House, Congressman John Quincy Adams took the floor to propose that the bill be sent to a thirteen-member select committee for consideration and recommendation. Such an unusual action was warranted, said Adams, by the state of civil war that existed between president and Congress. Several objected, pointing out that it was the job of Congress as a whole to reconsider vetoed bills. Adams' motion was, however, approved, 108–84. Of the thirteen committee members (including committee chairman Adams), eleven were anti-Tyler Whigs.

The following day, August 12, Congressman Irwin spoke in defense of Tyler's actions, expressing his shock over comments that they were provoking civil war between the two branches of government. Irwin made clear that his defense of Tyler was not predicated on mere politics, as he not only supported the tariff but opposed vigorous use of the veto (*Congressional Globe,* August 12, 1842: app., 832–33).

On August 16, 1842, Adams delivered the majority report of the committee, endorsed by ten of thirteen committee members (*Congressional Globe:* 894–901). The report first noted the accidental nature of Tyler's ascension to the presidency and the committee's view that the executive was separate from, yet dependent upon and responsible to Congress. Tyler's actions (his "executive legislation") were thus at loggerheads with this conception of executive-legislative relations.

In the case of the bill in question, Tyler had managed to thwart a bill vital to national interests; indeed, the bill was "prostrated, defeated, annulled, by the weak and wavering obstinacy of one man." The report surveyed Tyler's motives for this and his three other vetoes, concluding that "the whole legislative power of the Union has been, for the last fifteen months . . . in a state of suspended animation." Adams also mentioned the availability of the impeachment power, but surmised that the time for such an action was not right. The report concluded with the bitter complaint that the "power of the present Congress to enact laws essential to the welfare of the people has been struck with apoplexy by the executive hand" because of Tyler's stipulation that he would only sign a bill that conformed to his specifications. This, to a majority of the committee, was an "abusive exercise of the constitutional power of the President." The report recommended that the veto override be reduced to a simple majority.

Three committee members issued two separate reports in addition. Congressman Gilmer issued his own report, in which he questioned sending a vetoed bill to committee, as Congress was directed by the Constitution "to reconsider" vetoed bills. Gilmer then decried this attempt to, in his view, expand legislative power far beyond its appropriate scope. He referred also to dark invocations, heard during the time, of violence and 'revolution' as a response to the veto: "[I]t is now proclaimed that this power [the veto] is so dangerous to liberty as to justify an appeal to arms." Irwin argued that the president had not abused his power or assumed unwarranted prerogatives but that if he had, the appropriate mechanism for dealing with that was impeachment. Finally, Congress was presumptuous to condemn the president for what was essentially a difference of opinion.

Congressmen Ingersoll and Roosevelt also issued a dissenting report, in which they devoted much attention to the history and nature of the veto power. They pointed out that each house of Congress has an absolute veto on the other; that the courts exercise a veto when they strike down legislation; that a single member of Congress exercises a veto when a measure is defeated by a single vote. Thus, the 'one-man power' was, in a sense, pervasive in the governmental system. Moreover, the Constitution gives the president the veto as "the right which his conscience enjoins him to exercise." In this case, Tyler's objections "are contained in a respectful message, temperate in tone, persuasive in argument," and ultimately consonant with popular feeling.

With the submission of the report, the House was faced with two issues: the veto override itself, and the proposal to amend the Constitution. The former question was dealt with the following day, with the House voting to uphold the veto. Debate on both questions persisted for several days. Congressman Colquitt, for example, defended the necessity of the existing veto, and then turned his attention to "the bad temper manifested by the members of the Whig party." Examples of this "bad temper" cited by Colquitt included talk of revolution, anarchy, and assassination. In particular, he repeated Congressman Warren's comment in conversation "that, if he [Warren] saw the arm of the assassin raised to strike down John Tyler, he would not raise a finger to prevent it" (*Congressional Globe,* August 18, 1842: app., 813).

Congressman Rayner criticized the two minority reports but supported the proposal to amend the Constitution. Referring to Tyler repeatedly as the "acting President," he accused him of using the veto in a fashion unauthorized by the Constitution, and in a manner designed to enhance executive power. Rayner cited at some length excerpts from federal debate to show—seemingly at cross-purposes to his argument—that the founders principally feared legislative encroachments. He then argued that this fear was the primary motive for conferring the veto power. Thus, executive self-defense was viewed as not only the key reason for the veto but also as the principal cause for its use. Rayner went on to point out that the Constitution granted to Congress alone power of the purse. A presidential veto of a money bill thus violated the intent of the Constitution.

The referral of Tyler's fourth veto to committee did not pass the notice of the president. On August 30, he transmitted a message to the House protesting the violation of accepted procedure in the handling of the veto and the assault of his entire presidential record. Tyler's resolve seemed undiminished: "I am determined to uphold the Constitution . . . in defiance of all personal consequences" (*Messages,* 1913: III, 2046). The House refused to accept Tyler's message, however, and it was not entered in the *House Journal.*

A final constitutional card was played against the president on January 10, 1843 (*Congressional Globe:* 144–46). Tyler's archenemy, John Minor Botts, had made it clear during an exchange on the

House floor on July 6, 1842, that he was considering a formal move to impeach Tyler. Botts made good his promise the following January, during the third session of the Twenty-seventh Congress. Botts proposed a series of nine charges dealing with a laundry list of accusations. The two central charges were "withholding his assent to laws undispensable [*sic*] to the just operations of government" and "an arbitrary, despotic and corrupt abuse of the veto power." An additional count condemned Tyler for his so-called fifth veto, referring to Tyler's placing in State Department records his objections to part of a law, otherwise duly passed and signed, as an apparent circumvention of his presidential responsibility of seeing to the faithful execution of all laws. (This informal veto of a part of a law would also stir controversy when attempted by presidents in this century.) After some parliamentary maneuvering, the House voted on whether to refer the impeachment resolution to committee for consideration and recommendation. The vote failed, 83–127, killing the proposal. After the vote, several congressmen took the floor to condemn those Tyler critics who failed to support the move to impeach.

In the course of his administration, Tyler vetoed a total of ten bills, including four pocket vetoes. The pocket vetoes helped confirm the suspicion that Tyler had been converted to the Jacksonian mold (Jackson, 1967: 76). Tyler's last regular veto occurred on February 20, 1845, less than a month before he left office and long after the Whig Party had chosen another standard bearer. This final veto, involving a bill relating to revenue cutters and steamers, was historically significant because it was the first to be successfully overridden and enacted into law. Yet the override's political impact was, at best, inconsequential.[7] This fact highlights all the more the pivotal importance of Tyler's first four vetoes. Jackson (1967: 72) observes that "President Tyler's rejection of the bank and tariff bills represented the height of the veto power . . . because they [the vetoes] destroyed the very foundation of the Whig political program." Pious (1979: 64) argues a similar point about the Tyler vetoes when he notes that Tyler "had demonstrated conclusively that a president without a shred of popular or party support could wield prerogative power and by doing so reduce his congressional opponents to complete ineffectiveness in policymaking."

By all accounts, Tyler did not set out to either expand the bounds of his office or downplay congressional will. Rather, he was a staunch supporter of states' rights, and this fact guided his important veto decisions (Jackson, 1967: 73, 84). As to the bank issue, he had in fact made his views known before the 1840 election, though the desire of the Whigs to gain control of the government in that year resulted in the sublimation of this and other issue concerns. Tyler's states' rights orthodoxy combined with his artless political approach to produce the whirlwind surrounding the Twenty-seventh Congress. This turbulence was greatly enhanced by the manner of Tyler's ascension to office (and the attendent absence of an electoral mandate) and the fact that his use of the veto was inconsistent with the dominant philosophy of his own party. As some of the previous discussion reveals, the Whig view of the presidency was one of executive subordination to the legislative branch, as evidenced, for example, in their stated position that no president should serve more than one term. All of Tyler's vetoes, though especially the first four, were knives in the side of the Whiggish philosophy.

It is clear that the veto hurt Tyler in the eyes of Whig party leaders. However, Pious's observation above notwithstanding, Tyler's vetoes did find much support in the country. Various state legislatures and local governments passed resolutions of support, especially after the bank vetoes (e.g., *Senate document* 112 (27–1) 390; *Senate document* 118 (27–1) 390; *Senate document* 161 (27–3) 415; *Senate document* 94 (28–2) 451; *House document* 135 (28–2) 465; Jackson, 1967: 60–61, 63, 70–71). Had Tyler been willing and/or able to court sympathizers actively in both parties (he refused to jump parties or otherwise court the Democrats), he might well have gained some title to the Jacksonian legacy. Thus, despite the Whig Party position, Tyler's use of the veto had a certain popular appeal. Indeed, speaking in 1841, Supreme Court Justice Levi Woodbury equated the veto with presidential populism: "The veto power is the people's tribunative prerogative speaking again through their executive" (Ford, 1967: 187). This *vox populi* quality of the veto does much to explain the veto's symbolic and substantive role in enhancing the president's power. Its importance for the Jackson and Tyler presidencies—and, more important, for the precedents set by these two presidents—underscores the veto's vital (and early recognized) role in building a more powerful American presidency. Though this key role for the veto was recognized by observers of the time, it has gone largely ignored by modern analysts.

Finally, the Tyler presidency helped to inject the veto issue directly into party politics. This process began with the Jacksonian era, and was evidenced in the first written party platforms. The Democratic party platform of 1840 did not refer specifically to the veto, but it did mouth Jackson's assertions, reflected in his vetoes, that the Constitution did not grant the federal government the power to charter a national bank or finance internal improvements. In its presidential platforms from 1844 to 1856, the Democrats specifically defended the veto power, relying on nearly identical wording each time. The 1844 platform said this:

> [W]e are decidedly opposed to taking from the President the qualified veto power by which he is enabled, under restrictions and responsibilities amply sufficient to guard the public interest, to suspend the passage of a bill, whose merits cannot secure the approval of two-thirds of the Senate and House of Representatives, until the judgment of the people can be obtained thereon, and which has thrice saved the American People from the corrupt and tyrannical domination of the Bank of the United States. (Porter and Johnson, 1966: 4)

The Whigs never succeeded in contradicting the Democratic assertion of the veto as 'voice of the people.' The only reference to the veto to be found in the Whig platforms was a weak statement in 1844 calling for "a reform of executive usurpations" (Porter and Johnson, 1966: 9). In terms of their view of the presidency, the Whigs and their succeeding sympathizers fought a rear-guard action from Tyler on.

## Polk and the maturing veto

The relatively unpopular and stymied presidency of John Tyler was followed by the more popular and successful one of James K. Polk. Polk used the veto on three occasions. The first, delivered on August 3, 1846, was applied to a rivers and harbors bill. Like Jackson and other presidents, Polk questioned whether Congress had the constitutional authority to approve such internal improvements. He also found the bill inexpedient, especially as the country was at war with

Mexico, and needed its resources for this purpose. Debate in the House was relatively brief. Ironically (given past controversy over the veto), Polk was criticized for *not* announcing his intention to veto the bill before the fact (*Congressional Globe,* August 4, 1846: 1189). The veto was sustained, 96–91.

Polk's second veto came five days later, involving a bill to allow citizens to recover damages from French spoliations incurred during hostilities with the French before 1801. This issue had been a longstanding irritant. In his veto message, Polk made clear that this veto was rendered solely on the grounds of expediency: "I am truly sensible that it [the veto] should be an extreme case which would make it the duty of the Executive to withhold his approval of any bill passed by Congress upon the ground of its expediency alone. Such a case I consider this to be" (*Congressional Globe,* August 10, 1846: 1219).

In the Senate, several questioned the propriety of the veto. Senator Clayton said he thought it was the first veto in history based solely on expediency. He was of course wrong in this assertion. Nevertheless, he went on to assert that the founders never intended the veto to be used in a case of this sort. Senator Webster spoke similarly against the veto as "a new and alarming extension of Executive authority, not justified, not countenanced, finding no precedent, no apology, in any previous exercise of Executive power under this Constitution" (*Congressional Globe,* August 10, 1846: 1220). Yet even the great Webster's remarks were brief, and did not include any substantiation of his claims. Senator Benton delivered a lengthy and vigorous defense of the veto. Yet at no time did he feel the necessity to explain or defend the powers invoked by the president that stood behind the veto. This veto, too, was upheld, 27–15.

Polk's final veto, a pocket veto, also involved internal improvements; like the first veto, constitutional justification was invoked. Though not required to do so, Polk sent to Congress on December 15 an explanation for this March 3, 1847 veto. The message provoked debate in the House, including a proposal by Congressman Stewart that a special committee by appointed to examine the veto. No action was taken on the proposal, but the debate in Congress over internal improvements and the veto continued.

During the month of July, 1848, an intriguing and revealing debate unfolded in the House concerning a civil and diplomatic appropriations bill. This otherwise routine measure, designed to provide continuing funds for foreign ministers, judges, marshalls, and other civil officers, had been specifically recommended by Polk's administration. Yet word was passed to the House through Polk supporters that the president would veto the bill because the Ways and Means Committee had added to the bill three nongermane riders. The most controversial of these was an appropriation of fifty thousand dollars to dredge the Savannah River, which had been partly blocked by the Americans during the Revolutionary War to protect the city of Savannah from the British fleet. The wreckage left from the war had never been cleared and this hurt Savannah's competitive position as a shipping port. Georgia and the federal government had, up to this time, come to no agreement on who was to assume the cost of cleaning out the sunken wreckage.

Polk's stern opposition to this seemingly minor matter was founded in his belief, previously articulated in other vetoes, that the Congress lacked constitutional authority to deal with this. Polk's opponents bristled at the idea that the president would try to impose his imprint on legislation while it was still before Congress, and several stated unambiguously that the threat of a Polk veto would not alter their support of the appropriations bill, including the Savannah River project appropriation. Congressman Hudson, for example, proclaimed that he would "not deviate one-eighth of a hair from all the threats of Executive power which might be made" (*Congressional Globe,* July 20, 1848: 957). Several congressmen felt that Polk was using the veto to dictate his wishes to Congress and that this was a harbinger of the demise of separation of powers as well as a misuse of the veto power. Congressman Stephens accused Polk of doing "little else then trampling the Constitution beneath his feet" (*Congressional Globe,* July 20, 1848: 961). If the Congress were to buckle from presidential pressure, according to Congressman Smith, it "would be fit only to be the slaves of a despot, trembling at his presence, and shaping their votes to suit his views" (*Congressional Globe,* July 21, 1848: 966).

Whigs accused the Democrats of violating House rules (rule 81) prohibiting the attachment of nongermane riders. The Democrats responded that the action was consistent with the spirit of past legislative practices, as the Whigs had done the very same thing in 1842 to avoid a Tyler veto of a tariff bill that was tacked on to an important revenue bill. In the Tyler example the purpose was the same as the present case—to avoid a veto and enact the rider if possible; or, if a veto ensued, to use the veto to criticize the president publically (*Congressional Globe,* July 20, 1848: 957). Other examples of rider use were raised later in the debate (e.g., 980, 985).

Oft-heard criticisms of the veto were also raised—in particular, that it was monarchical, dictatorial, undemocratic, and that it was being used by Polk to make law and bend Congress to his will. Defenders argued that the veto was democratic, and that the president was, in fact, the truest voice of the people. Polk supporter Congressman Bayley argued that presidents such as Tyler were not only acting in accordance with the Constitution in exercising the veto, but would be committing *perjury* if they refrained from vetoing bills that they believed should be sent back to Congress. When asked to explain this novel position, Bayley quoted the constitutional phrase saying that the president "shall, from time to time, give to Congress information of the state of the Union, and recommend to their consideration such measures as he shall judge necessary and expedient." Bayley also quoted from the president's oath of office, wherein the president pledges to "faithfully execute the office of President . . . and . . . preserve, protect, and defend the Constitution." Therefore, if the president signs a bill he believes to be expedient, he is violating his constitutional duties as well as his oath of office. Bayley argued, too, that experience had shown that the political costs of veto use were considerable and that the president would therefore not employ the veto unless Congress had plainly contradicted public will. In thus exercising the veto, the president was acting as the country's truest representative of all the people (*Congressional Globe,* July 20, 1848: 957–60).

The seriousness of this debate was underscored by the fact that, by this time, Polk was a lame duck. The Democrats had turned their backs on Polk in favor of General Lewis Cass, and the Whigs had nominated General Zachary Taylor for president. The congressional debate thus included much speculation as to the stands of Cass and Taylor on the veto. At the conclusion of debate, the House passed the bill, including the Savannah River project, 108–78. No veto was applied.

The ability of a lame duck president to arouse such extended deliberations in the House reveals the already significant role of the president in the legislative process and the pivotal importance of the veto. The issues raised—control of Congress by the president, nongermane riders, veto threats, the political consequences of the veto for the president and Congress—are all issues of the veto today. In fact, with the most minor changes, this 1848 dispute could be easily mistaken for a contemporary one. Without doubt, the veto was coming of age.

Democrat Polk was succeeded by two Whigs, Zachary Taylor and Millard Fillmore. During the 1848 campaign, the veto was a major issue (Jackson, 1967: 99). Taylor made his views clear in his first annual message to Congress: "I view it [the veto] as an extreme measure, to be resorted to only in extraordinary cases, as where it may become necessary to defend the executive against the encroachments of the legislative power or to prevent hasty and inconsiderate or unconstitutional legislation" (*Messages,* 1913: III, 2561). After Taylor's death in 1850, Fillmore became president. In their collective four years in office, both subscribed to Whig principles by refraining from any use of the veto.

The veto returned in the presidencies of Franklin Pierce and James Buchanan. Most of the vetoes by both presidents involved internal improvement bills. Yet Pierce's argument that such measures were unconstitutional met with ever-more-forceful resistance because of the country's accelerating commerical expansion. This single trend primarily explains the fact that five of Pierce's nine vetoes were overridden. The overrides also support the assertion that successful vetoes must, at least in the perception of Congress, be backed by popular support.

Unlike vetoes of the previous decade, relatively little debate on the nature of the veto followed Pierce's applications of the power. Pierce's first veto, however, did engender a lengthy discussion of how soon an override vote needed to be taken after a bill was returned by the president. During consideration of two public works vetoes on July 7, 1856 (*Congressional Globe:* 1550), the chair of the Senate resolved the longstanding ambiguity of whether a successful veto override vote required two-thirds of *all* chamber members, or two-thirds of a *quorum* by ruling that the latter was appropriate (two-thirds of a quorum had been acceptable when Congress approved the Bill of Rights). The chair's ruling was upheld by the Senate, which overrode one of the vetoes by two-thirds of a quorum but less than two-thirds of the Senate's membership.[8]

Buchanan's seven vetoes were similarly conservative in conception. The fact that three were pocket vetoes probably prevented at least one of these from being overridden (Jackson, 1967: 108–10), and several of the bills vetoed by Buchanan were later enacted during Lincoln's term. The most damaging of Buchanan's vetoes was probably that of the popular Homestead Bill (enacted under Lincoln), which caused many northern farmers and laborers to turn away from the Democrats and support the new Republican party (Jackson, 1967: 112).

The Civil War–era presidents produced a large number of vetoes—seven by Lincoln and twenty-nine by Andrew Johnson. Although the vast majority of these were controversial in a political sense, they had little impact on the conception of the veto power itself. This conclusion stems from the simple fact that this was a time of national crisis, which therefore saw the circumvention of routine, noncrisis politics. One new twist emerged with Lincoln's first veto. For the first time, Congress took no override vote. Up to this time, the predominant interpretation had been that Congress was required to vote on a returned bill. After this time, Congress would often dispense with override attempts.

Lincoln's relative restraint in his use of the veto may be attributed to his willingness to compromise with Congress (Jackson, 1967: 115–16), the expanded powers he was able to exert during the Civil War, and perhaps his own Whig background. As a congressman, Lincoln wrote this about the veto: "Were I President, I should desire the legislation of the country to rest with Congress, uninfluenced by the executive in its origin or progress, and undisturbed by the veto unless a very special and clear case" (Sundquist, 1981: 24).

Andrew Johnson's twenty-nine vetoes set a numerical record. Like Tyler, Johnson ascended to the presidency through the death of the president. Also like Tyler, he was a high-minded constitutionalist who prided himself on his invocation of constitutional principles and precedents; in fact, he defended his constitutional interpretations "as though they had been transmitted from Sinai" (Corwin, 1957: 25). Like Tyler, he lacked basic political instincts. But unlike Tyler, he faced a Congress willing, able, and even eager to override his vetoes. If anything, the frequency of overrides accelerated the erosion of Johnson's political base. Of Johnson's twenty-one regular vetoes, fifteen were overridden.

By the end of Johnson's term, Congress was overriding his vetoes without debate and literally within minutes of their return to Congress. It was also true of Johnson that his vetoes helped fan the flames of impeachment. Unlike Tyler's case, however, the vetoes were themselves a relatively small component of the radical Republicans' grudge against Johnson; they came into play only because Johnson was impeached for violating provisions of laws he had initially vetoed. No charge of misuse of veto powers was made against Johnson in the articles of impeachment against him.

## The end of the veto controversy

The rise in use of the veto after the Civil War era was paralleled by a decline in objections about the basis of its use. Few of the many vetoes applied by presidents from Grant on aroused a level of controversy comparable to that surrounding controversial vetoes before the Civil War. And in the controversies that did arise there was a critical difference: Interpretations of the veto power rarely questioned the right of the president to veto any given bill if he considered it inappropriate to be a law. Presidential judgment continued to be questioned but not the power that gave rise to the judgment. As if to underscore this change in attitude, Congressman John Gear took the floor on March 1, 1889 (*Congressional Record:* 2556–57), during debate on a bill vetoed by President Cleveland. In a speech characterized as "somewhat unstable" (Jackson, 1967: 155), Gear invoked the arguments of Clay, Webster, and others to assert that the veto should only be used in extraordinary circumstances, and certainly not for reasons of expediency. Gear considered the veto to be an "alarming use of executive power." Yet by 1889, such arguments were anachronistic.

Several other important changes in the veto occurred after the Civil War. Aside from the vast increase in use (eighty-eight vetoes through 1868; over two thousand from then to the present), most vetoed bills were no longer subject to override attempts by the Congress. Some considered this a violation of the Constitution, but it saved much time and effort in the case of bills that did not possess adequate support. Presidents used the pocket veto more frequently, also without serious objection. Presidents began to rely more on cabinet officers and others for advice on whether to veto and for veto messages. Similarly, vetoed bills were more often referred to committees in Congress, where they often died. Finally, the principal cause for the proliferation of vetoes after the Civil War was the proliferation of private-pension and related private relief bills, of which more will be said.

Ambiguities over the precise nature of the veto power continued to give rise to problems. For example, in August, 1876, President Grant vetoed two bills but then informed Congress that he wished the bills returned to him, as he had changed his mind and now wished to sign them into law. In the instance of the first bill, a private relief measure, his request was ignored and no other action was taken on it. In the case of the second bill, involving a sale of Indian lands, the Senate openly rejected his request for return. Senator Sargent retorted that the president "has no more right to recall a bill after having vetoed it than he has . . . to tear a leaf out of the statute book" (*Congressional Record,* August 15, 1876: 5664). As if to endorse the point, the veto was overridden by both houses. Senator Sargent's reaction may have been the correct one constitutionally, but this is one of many such questions about the veto that has never been fully resolved.

The president and Congress came to political blows over the veto-related issue of attaching riders to legislation. The practice had occurred at least as early as the 1840s, but became far more frequent during the term of President Hayes. Several of his vetoes specifically involved appropriations bills (of which he approved) to which Congress had attached provisions politically objectionable to Hayes. In his veto messages, Hayes made his reasoning explicit. According to Hayes, the attachment of riders "strikes from the Constitution the qualified negative of the President." It also "will tend to destroy the equal independence of the several branches of the Government" (*Messages,* 1913: VI, 4483). Yet, as if to undercut his own assertion that riders rendered the veto ineffective, Hayes gained the upper hand in his struggle with Congress: He succeeded in forcing Congress to alter or strike out offending provisions by vetoing the bills that carried them. Among those bills he vetoed with objectionable riders, all were sustained. At the same time, however, he lost support within his party and became a one-term president.

## *Pensions, pork, and presidents*

As mentioned, the largest number of vetoed bills fell in the category of private pension bills. The pension system was widely (and correctly) perceived as corrupt. There was little incentive for members of Congress to reform the system, as they derived useful political capital by sponsoring the private pension requests of their constituents whether these were enacted or not. Indeed, congressmen often expected vetoes of suspect requests yet could be relatively sanguine about the outcome, as blame could be foisted on the president. Thus, the numerous private pension vetoes represented an intriguing political subsystem of request and refusal.

President Arthur summarized the political problem with keen understanding in an August 1, 1882 (*Messages,* 1913: VI, 4708) veto message: "As the citizens of one State find that money . . . is to be expended for local improvements in another State, they demand similar benefits for themselves. . . . Thus as the bill becomes more objectionable it secures more support." Both Presidents Arthur and Cleveland won reputations as protectors of the national purse through their use of the veto against private pension and other pork bills. Both were also extolled in Thomas Nast cartoons of the time. Though Arthur's vetoes amounted to only twelve, he was characterized as being "handy with his vetoes" (Jackson, 1967: 147). Arthur was also handicapped politically with the lack of an independent electoral mandate, as he ascended to the presidency through the death of James Garfield. Arthur's vetoes probably hurt his popularity, but they also served to extend the reputation of the president as the truest spokesman of national interest and as protector of the purse (see Fisher, 1972: 95). This public vision of the presidency found its fullest expression in the administration of Grover Cleveland.

In his first term of office, Cleveland vetoed exactly twice as many bills (414) as all of his predecessors combined. He vetoed another 170 bills in his second term. Of all these, only seven were overridden. On a single day in the summer of 1886, he was sent almost 240 private pension bills. In the month of June, 1886, he vetoed 56 bills. According to one account (Ford, 1921: 125), Cleveland was sent a total of 2042 private pension bills in his first term. Of these, most he signed, some he vetoed, but 284 became law without Cleveland's signature, indicating his unwillingness to affix his signature to bills he considered suspect.

Cleveland was not only handy with his vetoes but exercised some of them with a degree of sarcasm that enraged his opponents (Merrill, 1957: 106). In one case, a man who had served in the army for nine days during the final months of the Civil War contracted measles, was hospitalized, and then was released from the military. He applied for relief in 1880, claiming the measles had affected his eyes and back. Cleveland's veto message described the case this way: "Fifteen years after this brilliant service and this terrific encounter with the measles . . . the claimant discovered that his attack of the measles had some relation to his army enrollment" (*Messages,* 1913: VII, 5028).

The significance of Cleveland's prolific use of the veto should not be construed as merely a quantitative anomaly. First, the vetoes represented a major political preoccupation for the president and Congress (Parker, 1909: 99–100). *The Nation* (March 10, 1887: 202–3) observed that Cleveland "saved the Treasury from a tremem-dous onslaught of pension-beggars." Another observer of the time concluded that the federal government was "shaken to its very centre" by these and other disputes over the veto (Lockwood, 1884: 102). Second, the vetoes illustrated in the most public way possible the president's commitment to sound legislation and his advocacy of prudent use of national resources. Third, Cleveland's vetoes reflected his philosophy that the veto was and should be an integral component of his involvement in the legislative process. According to Cleveland, presidents reviewed legislation to "invoke the exercise of executive judgment, and invite independent executive action" (Beard, 1914: 614; Ford, 1921: 82).

Cleveland's politically aggressive use of the veto occurred in a period of political contentiousness—Ford (1921: 119) observes that Cleveland's "public life was passed under continual storm"—and all three of his presidential races were close contests. As with Hayes and Arthur, the veto clearly did not offer a ticket to instant political popularity. In fact, Cleveland's veto use probably cost him the election of 1888 (Jackson, 1967: 156; Fisher, 1972: 97). Yet the cumulative effect of these vetoes aided the advance of the strong presidency, in large part because of the very fact that this legislation involved 'distributive,' particularized benefits. According to one account of the time, most members of Congress lacked the influence to get legislation through Congress, as both chambers were controlled by a small clique. Thus, the best most members could hope for in terms of legislative accomplishment was to push through private pension bills for constituents. Congressmen labored to enact such bills, only to have many of them cut down by veto. The vetoes hurt congressmen of both parties by "turning to their injury what they had counted upon to help them in their districts" (Ford, 1921: 121), though they could still garner some benefit for having promoted such bills. This left the president as the de facto defender of the national treasury. The numerous vetoes provided ready evidence that the president was far more fiscally trustworthy than the Congress. In this way, the private-pension struggles led to one of the most important single acquisitions of presidential power: the granting to the executive of budget-making authority in the Budget and Accounting Act of 1921 (Fisher, 1972: 85–110).

### *The new view of the veto*

Without doubt, use of the veto in the late nineteenth century engendered controversy. But also without doubt, opposition to the veto was now based on political opposition arising from the particular issues of the time, rather than the questioning of presidential authority (Long, 1887: 254; Jackson, 1967: 155). A good example of the shift in veto debate (compared with that occurring before the Civil War) is seen in a speech, widely reprinted, by Congressman Randall Gibson, inspired by President Hayes's 1879 veto of an Army appropriations bill. Hayes had no objections to the appropriation itself but vetoed the bill because of a rider that would have repealed authorization to use federal troops at election polls to keep peace and avoid fraud. Apparently, Hayes had no great objection to the rider either but rather to the fact that it was lumped together with an appropriations bill. In his speech, Gibson (1879: 4, 7) conceded that the president could veto any bill "upon its merits." Gibson considered this veto, however, to be outside of the bounds of the presidential veto, because it was based "upon the ground that the methods adopted by this House are unconstitutional" (i.e. the attaching of nongermane riders). Since the internal procedures of each house are determined by each house alone and do not need presidential assent, the chief executive exceeds his authority by raising objections related to those procedures as a basis for a veto. Gibson's argument did not prevent the veto from being sustained; it did, however, exemplify the shifting nature of the veto debate.[9]

A political analyst writing after the peak of Cleveland's vetoes observed: "Notwithstanding the indignation which may be felt at some of President Cleveland's recent vetoes, I recollect no instance in which his authority to make them was seriously questioned" (Long, 1887: 254). Concomitant with the rising acceptance of the legitimacy of expansive use of the veto came recognition of its popular appeal. Long (1887: 257) also observed "that the veto of a bill is often the most efficient method of eliciting public sentiment." He shrewdly calculated its public value by noting that "the moment one man has set up his opinion against that of two or three hundred men, and has challenged the popular verdict as between himself and them, every one is interested." Note that Long is not saying that use of the veto automatically enhances the president's popularity but that it brings an issue more directly to the attention of the people. The consequences may damage the president's political standing, especially if most of the country already opposes him. Still, the president, in appealing directly to the country as a whole, sets himself up as its guardian and purveyor of the public interest. As Long said, "the veto becomes . . . an appeal to the people" (See also Bryce, 1891: I, 55). In this way, the veto emphasizes the fact that Congress, though close to the people, is composed of representatives of small, parochial constituencies, whereas the president alone possesses the single, national constituency.[10] In Cleveland's case, his vetoes "fixed the eyes of the country upon a gross perversion of Congressional energy" (Nevins, 1941: 328).

Cleveland's successor and predecessor, Benjamin Harrison, was somewhat more Whiggish in his attitude toward the presidency; he was also much more willing to accommodate himself to the wishes of Congress. Harrison's view of the veto was that it could be used on anything but that it should also be used parsimoniously and mostly on legislation possessing serious faults, or if the president wished to set precedent (Harrison, 1897: 133). Still, Harrison vetoed forty-four bills in four years; nearly all were distributive/private pension bills (as was also true of the vetoes of McKinley and Theodore Roosevelt).

This more prolific end-of-century veto use by no means simply created a strong presidency, but the veto did help pave the path to the modern public presidency. Nevertheless, the modern 'plebiscitary' presidency had not yet been fully realized by the close of the nineteenth century.[11] Bryce assessed presidential-congressional relations in 1891 (I, 223–4) by saying that Congress "has succeeded in occupying nearly all the ground which the Constitution left debatable between the President and itself." Bryce also noted that the "real strength of the executive therefore, the rampart from behind which it can resist the aggressions of the legislature, is in ordinary times the veto power."

### *The twentieth-century veto*

For American institutions, the current century has been the century of the presidency. Yet the veto power seemed to recede in importance, eclipsed by new powers, prerogatives, responsibilities, and crises. As historian Carlton Jackson (1967: 165) noted, during the McKinley and Theodore Roosevelt administrations, "the country was too involved in momentous struggles for world power and domestic reforms to be interested in presidential vetoes." The same could essentially be said of administrations of the next two presidents, William Howard Taft and Woodrow Wilson. Each used the veto without suffering serious criticism. Yet these two presidents are noteworthy for their thoughtful commentary on the veto power, and on the presidency generally, when not in office.

Taft took pride in his legal acumen and became Chief Justice of the United States after his term as president. In a series of lectures originally published in 1916, Taft (1967: 15–28) rejected the narrow interpretation of veto exercise, arguing instead its essential nature as part of the lawmaking process. He recognized also, though, that political tact often dictated less formal and public resolutions to presidential-congressional rifts that might otherwise result in a veto. Taft advanced, too, the argument that the president may well be the truest representative of the people as a whole, "freer from the influence of local prejudices." That this argument is made by Taft in his section on the veto underscores the close connection between the veto power and the presidential claim to being the people's first delegate. The objective truth of this claim is less significant than the degree to which the perception of its truth was and is pervasive. Taft also rejected as "utterly absurd" the veto-as-royal-prerogative epithet because of the president's elective ascension to office.

Before his presidency, political scientist and one-time president of the American Political Science Association, Woodrow Wilson rendered his thoughts on governmental powers in numerous writings. In *Congressional Government* (1956: 53, 173), Wilson called the veto the president's "most formidable prerogative" whereby the president "acts not as the executive but as a third branch of the legislature." For Wilson, the president "is no greater than his prerogative of veto makes him." These evaluations were offered in 1884, at a time when Congress was considered by most (including Wilson) to be the dominant national institution. Twenty-four years later, Wilson (1908: 54–81) recognized the growth of the presidency, but still acknowledged the vital role of the veto. In his eight years in office, Wilson did a great deal more than hand out vetoes. When subsequent presidents were otherwise less active, the veto emerged with greater visibility, as seen, for example, in Jackson's (1967: 187) assertion that Warren Harding's "most forceful presidential act" was his veto of the Soldier Bonus Bill in 1922.

The last president whose use of the veto seemed in some sense extraordinary was Franklin Roosevelt, who vetoed more bills (635) than any other president (though his average per year was less than that of Cleveland). Like Cleveland, the largest number of vetoes dealt with private pension/relief bills. Unlike Cleveland, however, Roosevelt dealt with Congresses that were, overall, supportive of his actions in a time when the president's menu of prerogatives was larger and still growing. Roosevelt's prolific use of the veto can be explained quite simply by the fact that, as one of history's greatest presidential activists, he used all of the tools available, including the veto (Burns, 1956: 186–87). As Neustadt (1954: 656) observed, FDR considered the veto to be "among the presidency's greatest attributes" and "a means of enforcing congressional and agency respect for presidential preferences or programs." In fact, the intriguing irony of his use of the veto is that, although it was usually a weapon of last resort, he could afford to use it more often precisely because he was dealing with a friendly and even submissive Congress. His famed "send me a bill I can veto" approach illustrates his recognition that the power has a positive as well as a negative function. FDR's appreciation of this facet of the veto was illustrated when, in 1935, he announced with great drama that he would deliver his veto of a veterans' bonus bill personally to a joint session of Congress. This unprecedented act was pure theater, designed to sway congressional, as well as popular sentiment (Roosevelt also delivered the veto address over national radio). The Senate voted to uphold the veto (Jackson, 1967: 210–11). FDR also relied heavily on the veto threat as a device for molding congressional action (Burns, 1956: 187). As important as the veto was to FDR, it was by now one of many powers. It was still important to modern presidents, but like a petunia in a bed of roses, it no longer attracted special notice.

## Conclusion

The presidential veto is inextricably linked to the changing nature of the presidency. In chapter 1, we observed the paring down of the powers of the English monarch, until the Crown was left only with the veto. In the American presidency, we observed the reverse phenomenon: the accumulation of presidential powers over legislative matters, beginning with the veto almost alone. The veto served as an important opportunity for presidents to exert greater influence over the legislative process (in particular as it advanced the ability of the president to involve himself in the legislative process before a bill reached his desk), first through the veto itself, then the veto threat, then anticipation by Congress of a veto threat, and thus to greater across-the-board consideration of the president's legislative and policy preferences by Congress. The veto was by no means the only avenue for greater presidential involvement in the legislative process, but its role was key and has certainly been underestimated. Moreover, the veto proved itself a potent weapon with its successful use as a deterrent, the rarity of successful veto overrides, and even its successful use against bills containing nongermane riders.

Given the fact that the overwhelming number of presidential vetoes in history involved 'distributive' bills (defined as those pertaining to particularized, concrete benefits such as public works and pension bills that can be dispensed and disaggregated unit by unit, also often labeled 'pork barrel' or 'patronage',[12] another important conclusion emerges. Since distributive legislation involves particularized benefits of importance to the members of Congress who originate them, presidents who vetoed such bills interfered with entrenched patronage patterns. Despite the very limited scope of many of these bills (especially private pension bills), the cumulative consequence of these vetoes represented a significant expenditure of the president's political resources (seen most clearly in President Cleveland's administration). On the other hand, presidents could also make political hay with the general public by holding up such vetoes as evidence of their attempt to protect the public purse from the greedy hands of special interests. The ability of presidents to promote themselves as protectors of the treasury found its clearest expression in the progressive transfer of budgetary authority to the president during the period from 1921 to the 1970s. Only in the last decade has Congress worked actively to reverse this presidential accumulation of power.

These long-term gains notwithstanding, individual presidents such as Buchanan, Grant, Hayes, and Cleveland encountered tough opposition and a barrage of criticism for some of their vetoes of distributive-type (and other) bills; it was opposition that depleted their limited political capital and left them vulnerable to counterattacks by opponents. Presidents who lacked an independent electoral mandate at the start, such as Tyler and Arthur, paid an even greater political price for their veto-related actions.

As mentioned at the beginning of this chapter, two presidents known for their veto use emerged from their presidencies no weaker and probably stronger for it, seeming to contradict the first half of the proposition that frequent veto use hurts presidents but helps the presidency. In the presidencies of Andrew Jackson and Franklin Roosevelt, both benefited from enormous and enduring grass-roots popularity (popularity that, unlike most, swelled over time (each gained a higher percent of the vote in his second election). In addition, each was considered to be a skilled leader, not only in Washington, but of the nation as a whole. Both presidents illustrate the axiom that a strong, popular president is best able to withstand the political fallout attendant on veto use. The irony is that a strong, resourceful president is least likely to need the veto, and the veto is otherwise still likely to be a weapon of last resort. Jackson used it precisely for its confrontational value. Roosevelt used it because he used everything. Among the other well-known activist presidents in history, none made special or prolific use of the veto in the context of his times. On the other hand, those presidents who relied principally on the veto, notably Tyler and Johnson, acquired a stigma of negativism inherent in their reliance on 'the negative'; that very reliance on the veto was prompted by both their weak initial political situations and inexpert political judgments.

With the evolution of the veto power came the ascendance of a key perception about it (and therefore about presidents as well): The veto is a people's power, exercised by the country's only nationally elected leader. There is surely a fine irony in the fact that the veto, derived from the monarchical check on representative assemblies, should be increasingly viewed as a kind of people's weapon, akin to the ancient Roman tribunal veto employed to protect the interests of the plebeians. In actual presidential use of the veto, there is some support for this assertion. Yet the *perception* that the 'tribunative prerogative' of the president represents the national interest over sectional, specialized interests in Congress is surely the most important fact, parallel as it is with this perception about the presidency as a whole. Bryce (1891: I, 55) observed that "far from exciting the displeasure of the people by resisting the will of their representatives, a President generally gains popularity by the bold use of his veto power." Writing shortly after Bryce, Henry Jones Ford (1967: 187) said "the veto power is sustained . . . by the representative character of the presidential office." The veto is "an instrument of popular control. Congress represents locality; the President represents the nation." Charles Beard (1914: 614) concluded similarly of the veto that "the people have come to regard it as a wholesome check upon a body [Congress] whose ways are sometimes regarded with suspicion, as lacking firmness in the face of sectional or private influences." Presidents who have tried to use the veto to its best political effect have often treated it as a plebiscitary device when the veto involved an important, or at least symbolically significant public issue. The classic, and perhaps earliest example was Jackson's veto of the bank bill in 1832, where that year's presidential election was viewed by both pro- and anti-Jackson forces as a plebiscite on the bank veto. Here again, even when such an appeal by the president did not prevail, it did contribute to the long-term view of the president as the nation's defender and promoter of the public interest.

In sum, the veto served at least three important functions in contributing to the modern presidency: (1) It served as a key vehicle for direct appeal to the public; (2) it had a certain cumulative deterrent effect on Congress influencing the congressional agenda as presidents became more bold in their use of the veto and the veto threat; and

(3) its use succeeded over time in rolling back the perceived limitations on veto use (though such limitations are not found in the Constitution). Over time, presidents succeeded in neutralizing claims that the veto could only be used rarely or only for constitutional reasons or that the president should not announce his preferences while Congress was still considering a bill. The days when a president could face impeachment charges or open threats of death for a mere veto are entirely removed from the presidential experience today. That this is so is a remarkable commentary on how far the presidency has evolved in a century and on the role played by the veto in that process.

# 3

# The Modern Veto

*Among the substantial objections to the great powers of the president, that of his* negative *upon the laws, is one of the most inconsiderable. . . . For, if he be a bold enterprising fellow, there is little fear of his ever having to exercise it. . . . [I]f, however, I say, he should not be a man of an enterprising spirit, in that case he will be a* minion *of the aristocratics, doing according to their will and pleasure, and confirming every law they may think proper to make.*

Antifederalist Philadelphiansis
see Storing (1981)

Students of the presidency often segment the institution into historical eras to denote important changes in structure and power. Yet such segmentation ought not to hide the simple, overriding reality that the current presidency is the logical, even inexorable extension of its own past history. One need only trace the development of the presidential veto to see how the antecedents and development of the power led to its contemporary form.

## A summary assessment

A logical entry to consideration of the modern veto begins with a summary examination of the records of our first thirty-nine presidents. Table 3.1 offers a version of the summary most often reprinted in textbooks on the presidency, though it also includes a calculation of vetoes per year for each president. By itself, this information reveals

## Table 3–1
## Summary of Bills Vetoed, 1789–1987 [a]

| *President* | *Total vetoes* | *Regular vetoes* | *Pocket vetoes* | *Vetoes per year* [b] | *Vetoes overridden* |
|---|---|---|---|---|---|
| George Washington | 2 | 2 | — | .2 | — |
| John Adams | 0 | — | — | — | — |
| Thomas Jefferson | 0 | — | — | — | — |
| James Madison | 7 | 5 | 2 | .9 | — |
| James Monroe | 1 | 1 | — | .1 | — |
| John Q. Adams | 0 | — | — | — | — |
| Andrew Jackson | 12 | 5 | 7 | 1.5 | — |
| Martin Van Buren | 1 | — | 1 | .2 | — |
| W. H. Harrison | 0 | — | — | — | — |
| John Tyler | 10 | 6 | 4 | 2.5 | 1 |
| James K. Polk | 3 | 2 | 1 | .7 | — |
| Zachary Taylor | 0 | — | — | — | — |
| Millard Fillmore | 0 | — | — | — | — |
| Franklin Pierce | 9 | 9 | — | 2.2 | 5 |
| James Buchanan | 7 | 4 | 3 | 1.7 | — |
| Abraham Lincoln | 7 | 2 | 5 | 1.7 | — |
| Andrew Johnson | 29 | 21 | 8 | 7.2 | 15 |
| Ulysses S. Grant | 93 | 45 | 48 | 11.6 | 4 |
| Rutherford B. Hayes | 13 | 12 | 1 | 3.2 | 1 |
| James A. Garfield | 0 | — | — | — | — |
| Chester A. Arthur | 12 | 4 | 8 | 3.0 | 1 |
| Grover Cleveland | 414 | 304 | 110 | 103.5 | 2 |
| Benjamin Harrison | 44 | 19 | 25 | 11.0 | 1 |
| Grover Cleveland | 170 | 42 | 128 | 42.5 | 5 |
| William McKinley | 42 | 6 | 36 | 10.5 | — |
| Theodore Roosevelt | 82 | 42 | 40 | 10.2 | 1 |
| William H. Taft | 39 | 30 | 9 | 9.7 | 1 |
| Woodrow Wilson | 44 | 33 | 11 | 5.5 | 6 |
| Warren G. Harding | 6 | 5 | 1 | 3.0 | — |
| Calvin Coolidge | 50 | 20 | 30 | 8.3 | 4 |
| Herbert Hoover | 37 | 21 | 16 | 9.2 | 3 |
| Franklin D. Roosevelt | 635 | 372 | 263 | 52.9 | 9 |
| Harry S. Truman | 250 | 180 | 70 | 31.2 | 12 |
| Dwight D. Eisenhower | 181 | 73 | 108 | 22.6 | 2 |
| John F. Kennedy | 21 | 12 | 9 | 10.5 | — |
| Lyndon B. Johnson | 30 | 16 | 14 | 5.0 | — |
| Richard M. Nixon | 43 | 26 | 17 | 7.8 | 7 |
| Gerald R. Ford | 66 | 48 | 18 | 26.4 | 12 |
| Jimmy Carter | 31 | 13 | 18 | 7.7 | 2 |
| Ronald Reagan (1981–1987) | 62 | 33 | 29 | 8.9 | 8 |
| Total | 2453 | 1413 | 1040 | | 102 |

[a] Data drawn from *Presidential Vetoes, 1789–1976, 1977–1984,* and update from U.S. Senate Library.

[b] Rounded to the nearest tenth. For those presidents who did not serve full years, their years in office were rounded to match the nearest complete Congress, since vetoes can only be exercised when Congress is in session.

relatively little aside from the distinction between regular vetoes, subject to congressional override, and pocket vetoes, which cannot be overridden. Table 3.2 is much more revealing. First, it is clear that most vetoes (1544) have been of private bills, whereas 909 public bills have been vetoed. Private bills have not been widely vetoed since Eisenhower's term (private bills will be discussed more extensively later in the chapter). Of even greater significance is the fact that the overwhelming number of successful congressional overrides have been of public bills. This is entirely logical, since a bill would almost have to involve a significant public issue for it to attract the two-thirds majority in both houses necessary for a successful override. Private bills, by definition, are extremely narrow in scope; indeed, only one private-bill veto has been overridden in this century.

As noted at the bottom of table 3.2, 7.2 percent of all regular, non–pocket vetoes have been overridden (it makes no sense to include in the equation pocket vetoes—though this is often done—as they are not returned to Congress). Yet when we consider public and private regular vetoes separately in terms of override, we note that 19.3 percent of all public-bill vetoes subject to override have in fact been overridden; only 0.8 percent of private-bill vetoes have been overridden. Naturally, these figures are not evenly distributed across the thirty-nine presidents, but they are still important as a summary assessment of the presidential veto record, especially in relation to the fate of public-bill vetoes. A .807 batting average is still very respectable (and of course most overrides are accounted for by a handful of presidents), but clearly the veto when applied to public bills is not omnipotent. The final column of overrides as a percent of regular vetoes generally reinforces the historical account of the last chapter.

Table 3.3 ranks presidents by their average veto use. It is of interest as a simple scorecard of how frequently the thirty-nine presidents used the veto. It would be a mistake to interpret too much from this and the other tables, however, since they take no account of historical era and circumstance. The principal interest of this study is not who took the largest number of metaphorical swings at the presidential plate (though frequency is of some importance), but rather how the power has evolved. The importance of Tyler's ten vetoes, Washington's two vetoes, and Monroe's one veto, for example, is far greater than the simple numerical ranking would imply. It is for this

**Table 3–2**
**Regular and Pocket Vetoes for Public and Private Bills, and Overrides, 1789–1987** [a]

| *President* | *Regular Vetoes* | | *Pocket Vetoes* | | *Overrides* | | *Overrides as percent of regular vetoes* |
|---|---|---|---|---|---|---|---|
| | *Public* | *Private* | *Public* | *Private* | *Public* | *Private* | |
| George Washington | 2 | 0 | 0 | 0 | — | — | — |
| John Adams | 0 | 0 | 0 | 0 | — | — | — |
| Thomas Jefferson | 0 | 0 | 0 | 0 | — | — | — |
| James Madison | 3 | 2 | 2 | 0 | — | — | — |
| James Monroe | 1 | 0 | 0 | 0 | — | — | — |
| John Q. Adams | 0 | 0 | 0 | 0 | — | — | — |
| Andrew Jackson | 5 | 0 | 7 | 0 | — | — | — |
| Martin Van Buren | 1 | 0 | 0 | 0 | — | — | — |
| W. H. Harrison | 0 | 0 | 0 | 0 | — | — | — |
| John Tyler | 6 | 0 | 4 | 0 | 1 | — | 16.7 |
| James K. Polk | 2 | 0 | 1 | 0 | — | — | — |
| Zachary Taylor | 0 | 0 | 0 | 0 | — | — | — |
| Millard Fillmore | 0 | 0 | 0 | 0 | — | — | — |
| Franklin Pierce | 9 | 0 | 0 | 0 | 5 | — | 55.6 |
| James Buchanan | 2 | 2 | 3 | 0 | — | — | — |
| Abraham Lincoln | 2 | 0 | 4 | 1 | — | — | — |
| Andrew Johnson | 21 | 0 | 6 | 2 | 15 | — | 71.4 |
| Ulysses S. Grant | 16 | 29 | 37 | 11 | 1 | 3 | 8.9 |
| Rutherford B. Hayes | 11 | 1 | 1 | 0 | 1 | — | 9.0 |
| James A. Garfield | 0 | 0 | 0 | 0 | — | — | — |
| Chester A. Arthur | 3 | 1 | 0 | 8 | 1 | — | 25.0 |
| Grover Cleveland | 33 | 271 | 28 | 82 | 1 | 1 | .7 |
| Benjamin Harrison | 14 | 5 | 2 | 23 | 1 | — | 5.3 |
| Grover Cleveland | 12 | 30 | 29 | 99 | 3 | 2 | 11.9 |
| William McKinley | 2 | 4 | 4 | 32 | — | — | — |
| Theodore Roosevelt | 15 | 27 | 9 | 31 | 1 | — | 2.4 |
| William H. Taft | 20 | 10 | 2 | 7 | 1 | — | 3.3 |
| Woodrow Wilson | 26 | 7 | 9 | 2 | 6 | — | 18.2 |
| Warren G. Harding | 2 | 3 | 1 | 0 | — | — | — |
| Calvin Coolidge | 17 | 3 | 13 | 17 | 4 | — | 20.0 |
| Herbert Hoover | 17 | 4 | 10 | 6 | 3 | — | 14.3 |
| Franklin D. Roosevelt | 55 | 317 | 83 | 180 | 9 | — | 2.4 |
| Harry S. Truman | 43 | 137 | 32 | 38 | 11 | 1 | 6.7 |
| Dwight D. Eisenhower | 30 | 43 | 44 | 64 | 2 | — | 2.7 |
| John F. Kennedy | 4 | 8 | 5 | 4 | — | — | — |
| Lyndon B. Johnson | 4 | 12 | 10 | 4 | — | — | — |
| Richard M. Nixon | 26 | 0 | 14 | 3 | 7 | — | 26.9 |
| Gerald R. Ford | 45 | 3 | 16 | 2 | 12 | — | 25.0 |
| Jimmy Carter | 13 | 0 | 16 | 2 | 2 | — | 15.4 |
| Ronald Reagan (1981–1987) | 31 | 2 | 24 | 5 | 8 | — | 24.2 |
| Total | 493 | 921 | 416 | 623 | 95 | 7 | |

[a] Information drawn from Berdahl (1937); *Presidential Vetoes, 1789–1976, 1977–1984,* and update from U.S. Senate Library. Of all regular, non-pocket vetoes, 7.2% have been overridden successfully; of all public bill non-pocket vetoes, 19.3% have been overridden; of all private bill non-pocket vetoes, 0.8% have been overridden.

reason that these and other earlier vetoes received special attention in chapter 2.

## Empirical assessments

Few dispute the continuing importance of the modern presidential veto power. At the same time, however, it has seemingly played a relatively small role in the administrations of modern presidents. This parallels a similar scholarly paradox, wherein scholars and other analysts continue to recognize the importance of the veto power (e.g. Binkley, 1958; Finer, 1960; Pessen, 1975; Black, 1976; Wayne, 1978; Sundquist, 1986), yet give it little scholarly attention. The short answer to this apparent contradiction is the one suggested in the previous chapter: The veto power is still important, but it has been eclipsed by other, more recently acquired powers and prerogatives, especially the president's greatly expanded role in budget-making and the legislative process. Adequate understanding of the veto power does not end with this assertion, but rather begins with it.

**Table 3–3**
**Presidents Ranked by Veto Use** [a]

| President | Average | President | Average |
|---|---|---|---|
| 1. Cleveland (1st term) | 103.5 | 21. L. Johnson | 5.0 |
| 2. Cleveland (both terms) | 73.0 | 22. Hayes | 3.2 |
| 3. F. Roosevelt | 52.9 | 23. Arthur | 3.0 |
| 4. Cleveland (2d term) | 42.5 | 24. Harding | 3.0 |
| 5. Truman | 31.2 | 25. Tyler | 2.5 |
| 6. Ford | 26.4 | 26. Pierce | 2.2 |
| 7. Eisenhower | 22.6 | 27. Buchanan | 1.7 |
| 8. Grant | 11.6 | 28. Lincoln | 1.7 |
| 9. B. Harrison | 11.0 | 29. Jackson | 1.5 |
| 10. McKinley | 10.5 | 30. Madison | .9 |
| 11. Kennedy | 10.5 | 31. Polk | .7 |
| 12. T. Roosevelt | 10.2 | 32. Van Buren | .2 |
| 13. Taft | 9.7 | 33. Washington | .2 |
| 14. Hoover | 9.2 | 34. Monroe | .1 |
| 15. Reagan (1981–1987) | 8.9 | 35. J. Adams | 0 |
| 16. Coolidge | 8.3 | 36. Jefferson | 0 |
| 17. Nixon | 7.8 | 37. J. Q. Adams | 0 |
| 18. Carter | 7.7 | 38. W. Harrison | 0 |
| 19. A. Johnson | 7.2 | 39. Taylor | 0 |
| 20. Wilson | 5.5 | 40. Fillmore | 0 |
| | | 41. Garfield | 0 |

[a] Figures given are yearly averages.

### *Determinants of veto use*

As has been observed about the presidency (Heclo, 1977; Shull, 1979; Spitzer, 1983), few readily quantifiable indicators present themselves to aid the study of this institution. The veto is an exception. Yet the exceptional nature of the veto act itself has probably discouraged greater attention to it, leaving only a few, usually narrow and limited studies focused on the veto. A 1975 study (Lee) sought to analyze the frequency of presidential vetoes to determine the circumstances under which vetoes are most likely to occur. This study concluded that several factors are related to the likelihood of veto use by a president. A veto is more likely if the president and Congress are controlled by different parties, if the president is a Democrat (the two most prolific users of the veto were Democrats), and if the president has a higher electoral vote total. A veto is less likely the more years a president has spent in Congress before becoming president. Congress is more likely to override a veto when party control is split between the two branches, when electoral support for the president is low, after a midterm election (the president's party usually loses seats in Congress in midterm elections), and in times of economic crisis. Congress is less likely to override in times of war or military crisis. These conclusions are intuitively as well as empirically plausible, and the historical account of the last chapter endorses nearly all of these tendencies. The study also concluded that strong presidents are not necessarily veto presidents.

A revision of this study (Copeland, 1983) confirmed some results but contradicted others. It found that the veto is more likely when party control of one branch is different from that of the other, when the president possesses a stronger electoral mandate, and when the president lacks experience in Congress. Copeland also found that when the role of government expanded, so too did use of the veto; also, the more veto overrides a president encounters, the less likely he is to use the veto. Vetoes are also more frequent during the president's second and fourth years of his term. In contrast with Lee, however, Copeland concluded that Democratic presidents are not more likely to use the veto than Republicans (the results in Lee's study having been skewed by Democrats Franklin Roosevelt and Grover Cleveland) and that the presence of economic and military crises also have no impact.

These first two studies examined the vetoes of all presidents. Yet studies of presidential vetoes since the World Warr II era yield findings that conform to broader historical patterns. Ringelstein (1985) found no important differences between the vetoes of Republicans and Democrats from Eisenhower to the present. When Republicans did veto more often, it was because they faced a hostile Congress. Ringelstein observed few vetoes of foreign policy bills, explainable by the president's greater influence over this policy area. Most importantly, the study concluded that "the categories of and reasons for presidential vetoes are remarkably similar from president to president . . . they seem to have just as much in common as presidents doing battle with Congress than as Republicans and Democrats fighting for differing ideological programs and considerations" (Ringelstein, 1985: 52–53). This held generally for the justifications of vetoes by presidents and the subject matter of the bills.

A study by Rohde and Simon (1985) worked with essentially the same set of factors analyzed in prior empirical studies, but formulated a presidential veto model using simulations. They broke the veto process into three successive stages: the veto decision, the override attempt, and the success of the attempt. The efficacy of the president's actions and the congressional reaction hinged on the political environment and prevailing resources. Despite the greater complexity of the approach, the findings paralleled previous studies. In particular, public support was seen as vital for the success of presidential vetoes as well as congressional overrides. They found, too, that when public support for presidents eroded, use of the veto was more likely—yet, so too, was the likelihood of failure. Similarly, a veto is most potent at the time when it is least needed—at the beginning of an administration. This conforms to Neustadt's (1980: 67) observation that the "weaker his [the president's] apparent popular support, the more his cause in Congress may depend on negatives at his disposal, like the veto."

Some of the political consequences of the veto addressed by these more quantitative studies were also addressed in a case study of veto override politics during the Reagan administration. This analysis of Congress's first successful override of a Reagan veto, involving a $14.2 billion supplemental appropriations bill, identified constraints that limit the ability of the president to influence Congress on a veto override. Levine (1983) noted in this case a phenomenon often found, ironically, during times when the president's influence over Congress is especially great (as it was for Reagan in 1982): the sense among legislators that they needed to demonstrate some independence and assertiveness and that they were not simply 'Reagan robots.' Levine found that Reagan did not lay the early groundowrk necessary for sustaining his veto. This was not an oversight, however; it occurred because the administration was waiting to see what form the bill would finally take. To sustain the veto, Reagan needed support from some congressmen who had initially supported the bill. It was difficult to get such switchover votes, however, when key congressmen could not be informed early of an impending veto. The president is also constrained to lobby only the chamber that receives back from the president the vetoed bill, as pressure applied to both chambers is perceived as a sign of presidential weakness (such broad lobbying presupposes that the president may lose the first override vote, and this impression may erode support for the president's position). Above all, the case illustrates that use of the veto has significant political costs. Even a strong, popular president must lay careful groundwork and account for congressional sensibilities. A president who does not do this faces the prospect of strong congressional backlash.

## Central clearance and the enrolled bill process

As the discussion in chapter 2 illustrated, presidents since George Washington have sought advice on whether to veto bills. Such advice was often sought from cabinet secretaries and department heads affected by the legislation in question and would often include a request for a draft veto message. But as the presidency became institutionalized in the twentieth century, so too did the handling of veto decisions.

The drive to institutionalize the veto process was impelled by one overriding force: the constitutionally mandated ten-day period in which to sign or veto a bill. When an enrolled bill (one passed by Congress, but not yet signed into law) reached the White House, a presidential aide would guess which agency or agencies would be affected, have the bill hand delivered to them, and then wait for a reply. This process often yielded inadequate, ill-considered veto decisions (as happened, notably, during Cleveland's terms).

The process of dealing more systematically and effectively with enrolled bills and possible vetoes began to acquire greater coherence with the creation of the Bureau of the Budget (BOB; known as Office of Management and Budget after 1970) in 1921. The Budget Bureau was asked to render its views of enrolled appropriations bills as part of the larger attempt to enhance executive authority over the budget process. Naturally, this led to occasional veto recommendations from the BOB.

This examination of enrolled bills was expanded by Franklin Roosevelt in 1934 to include private bills. Soon, the White House was sending all varieties of enrolled bills to the BOB, requesting that they contact the appropriate departments and summarize prevailing views about the legislation. By 1938, the BOB had assumed this responsibility for virtually all bills. The Budget Bureau also succeeded in getting early printings of enrolled bills so that they could be distributed to appropriate agencies even before they reached the president. In 1939, the BOB issued a circular that identified it as the president's official agent in dealing with all enrolled bills; when agencies were requested to provide information, they were obliged to respond within forty-eight hours. The response was to include a specific recommendation. If the recommendation was negative, a draft veto message (or memorandum of disapproval, in the case of pocket vetoes) was to be forwarded. From this point forward, the handling of possible vetoes was systemized and bureaucratized (Neustadt, 1954: 654–56).

Since the 1930s, this handling of bills has changed relatively little; it has also maintained one overriding concern: considering all legislation in the light of the president's legislative program. One of the first acts of the Legislative Reference Division (that part of the Office of Management and Budget responsible for dealing with enrolled bills) is to draft a memorandum summarizing the background, purposes, and relation of the bill to the president's program. The memorandum also summarizes the president's options. Written agency responses are also appended. This packet of information (the 'enrolled bill file') is then sent on to the White House, usually by the fifth day of the ten-day period, where presidential aides add their recommendations to assist the president in his final determination. White House aides are more inclined than the OMB or other agencies to have the president's immediate, political needs in mind (Wayne and Hyde, 1978).

From the Roosevelt period to about 1965, the Budget Bureau tried to avoid overt political considerations in its recommendations, concerning itself more directly with budgetary limitations and the objective merits of bills. Because of the volume of legislation, Budget Bureau recommendations carried considerable weight, as did those of the career civil servants within the bureau who assumed the brunt of the work. Toward the end of his term, however, President Johnson created a new political-level position at the bureau. This appointment marked the beginning of a process of greater general politicization in the Budget Bureau, and therefore in its handling of possible vetoes. Under Nixon, the BOB was reconstituted as the OMB. Among the changes was the creation of four politically appointed associate directors who assumed key responsibilities. As a consequence, the assessment of enrolled bills came under the purview of political appointees rather than civil servants. Still, the basic mechanisms established in the 1930s continued to operate regardless of political tides. Even during the Watergate period in 1974, the OMB continued to operate without interruption. Also during this period, White House staff resources devoted to the consideration of enrolled bills were increased and formalized. Despite this, however, the OMB continued to exert decisive influence (Wayne and Hyde, 1978).

An important study (Wayne, Cole, and Hyde, 1979) examined the enrolled bill memoranda prepared by the OMB during the Nixon and Ford presidencies to assess influence over the decision of the president to sign or veto bills. Focusing on more important, controversial bills, the study found that OMB recommendations had the greatest impact on the president's decision to veto, followed by the recommendations of the lead agency (that most directly affected by the bill), though the OMB recommendation is often influenced by the recommendation of the lead agency. An OMB recommendation to veto does not, however, assure a veto, though vetoes rarely occur when the OMB does not recommend such action. This is attributable to the White House's continued reliance on the OMB's expertise, but also to the fact that the OMB is more politicized, and thus more responsive to the president's political needs to begin with (Wayne and Hyde, 1978: 293). The politicization of the OMB has accelerated during the Reagan administration.[1] To the extent that OMB recommendations to veto are not followed by presidents, it is attributable to the general bias in favor of signing legislation, other things being equal.

## Private bills and the veto

The data previously presented reveal that about sixty-three percent of all vetoes involve private bills. Yet little or no public attention is paid today to private legislation—understandable in principle, since by definition it does not involve public policy, but matters of very narrow and parochial concern. According to the *U.S. Code,* private bills are defined as "all bills for the relief of private parties, bills granting pensions, bills removing political disabilities, and bills for the survey of rivers and harbors" ("Private Bills," 1966: 1684). Private bills usually deal with relief, pensions, or claims of named individuals or other specific entities, such as corporations.

The pertinent questions regarding private bills are these: (1) why have there been more private than public-bill vetoes? (2) what accounts for the fact that a private-bill veto is more than twenty times as likely to be sustained than that of a public bill? and (3) are private-bill vetoes handled any differently than those of public bills? The first question is the simplest. Most private-bill vetoes (about two-thirds, see table 3.2) occurred in three administrations—Cleveland, Franklin Roosevelt, and Truman—as the result of war-related pension and other claims. The claims were the subject of significant public attention, especially during the Cleveland era (see chapter 2). The other two questions require some veto history review.

From roughly the beginning of this century, the procedures for handling private-bill vetoes diverged from those for public bills. At the start of the Republic, no distinction was made in the treatment of public and private bills. The first two vetoes of private bills, by President Madison, occurred in 1811. Although procedures for handling the vetoed bills were discussed on the floor of Congress, there was no suggestion that the bills' treatments should differ because they were private. The next private-bill veto occurred in 1860. This time, however, an argument unsubstantiated by law or past practice was promoted on the floor of the Senate, proposing that, since the private bill in question involved a matter of mere money (the bill was to provide relief for several men seeking compensation for mail transport) instead of policy, it ought to be referred to committee instead of considered by the full chamber, as was the practice of the time. The attempt to refer the bill failed, but the principle that private-bill vetoes should be handled differently found greater support as time went on (Berdahl, 1937: 516–19).

Although the right of the president to veto private bills was questioned by some members of Congress, especially at the end of the nineteenth century, actual practice has resulted not only in a thorough refutation of this argument but in a situation where presidential vetoes of private bills almost invariably prevail. This is seen in the expeditious reconsideration in Congress of vetoed public bills (though Congress may decide to take no action, or to postpone a vote), whereas vetoed private bills are typically not dealt with at all. Instead, these bills are usually referred back to committee, from whence they rarely emerge.

The reasons for the lack of critical attention to vetoed private bills are fairly obvious. First, congressional workload is such that most members can hardly be bothered when another congressman's private bill is vetoed. As Berdahl (1937: 531) observes, private bills "are passed in default of serious opposition rather than because of enthusiastic affirmative support." Unanimous consent was and is the order of the day for passage of such bills. Second, private bills are submitted to assessment by appropriate executive departments and agencies after passage as part of the enrolled bill process. When the recommendation to veto emerges and is implemented, it is perceived, in many ways, as a nonpartisan judgment, unlike most public-bill vetoes. The reasons cited by presidents for these vetoes invariably include "unjustifiably favored treatment for an individual" ("Private Bills," 1966: 1701). Concern is also often raised that a given private bill would set an inappropriate precedent. These relatively narrow concerns merely enhance the likelihood that Congress will defer to the president. To cite one such example, when Franklin Roosevelt vetoed in 1936 a private bill that had initially passed unanimously in one house and by a large majority in the other, the vote to override (forced by the bill sponsor) resulted in a near-unanimous vote in support of Roosevelt (Berdahl, 1937: 528–31). The unwillingness of Congress to reconsider private-bill vetoes is altered only in the instance of a change in facts or written evidence that the administration has changed its mind on the bill in question. The only other avenue for the persistent congressional sponsor who finds his or her private bill vetoed is to reintroduce it. Some claims do, in fact, persist for many years ("Private Bills," 1966: 1692–93).

Finally, it is important to note that the handling of private bills has changed little in the last fifty years, and that very few have been vetoed since the 1950s. But the contemporary lack of interest in and concern about private bills could change, as it has in our past, should circumstances prompt an increase in their introduction and passage, as in the aftermath of a war.

## The veto in the hands of modern presidents

### *Truman*

Despite the fact that the veto power is now but one of many presidential prerogatives enforcing executive preeminence over legislative affairs, recent presidents have continued to recognize its importance. President Truman, for example, used the veto against many major bills, the most well known being the Taft-Hartley Act of 1947 (enacted into law over his veto). Speaking of the veto power, Truman called it "one of the most important instruments of his authority." He viewed the veto message as "an opportunity to set forth clearly and in detail . . . the policies of his administration" (Finer, 1960: 75). Truman claimed to have given veto messages more of his attention than any other White House pronouncements.

### *Eisenhower*

Eisenhower also recognized the importance of the veto—a realization enhanced, no doubt (as it was for Truman), by the prospect of dealing with an often hostile and contentious Congress. As with so many of his predecessors, Eisenhower proclaimed that he applied the veto for, and on behalf of, the public good. Though he did not use it lightly, Eisenhower did use it, notably, to 'subdue' the Democratic Congress of 1958–59 (Finer, 1960: 58, 76).

### *Kennedy and Johnson*

Eisenhower's two Democratic successors employed the veto far less than their predecessors. Not surprisingly, they also faced Congresses that were far more compliant; thus, they had less occasion to use the weapon of last resort. The veto was still applied, given the Rooseveltian lesson that a president dealing from strength can afford the political costs of the veto far better than a president buffaloed by a cantankerous Congress. As an aide to Lyndon Johnson noted, "It is inevitable that the President will use the veto at some point. It's the best method to show the Congress he means business" (Light, 1982: 111). When these two Democrats did use the veto, they took particular care that their vetoes not be overridden. "Indeed, to have a Democratic Congress override a Democratic president's veto would have been a source of great embarrassment" (Wayne, 1978: 149). An aide to Kennedy offered this telling insight into that administration's recognition of the limitations of the veto: "There is always some pressure to attack Congress when you are losing; always some advice to bring the veto down hard. However, if the President wants to accomplish anything, he has to present positive proposals. He has to make a mark on the legislative calendar" (Light, 1982: 112). These observations reveal again that the veto cannot be taken lightly as a political weapon, regardless of the president's circumstances, and that the costs of its prolific use are high, especially if not counterbalanced with positive alternatives (e.g. Hinckley, 1985: 161).

During the period of the presidencies of Nixon through Reagan, the veto reemerged, in large part as a measure of greater presidential-congressional contentiousness and partisan acrimony. From 1969 to 1988, the same political party controlled the presidency and both houses of Congress only during Carter's four years. As Hargrove and Nelson (1984: 208–9), among others, observe, modern presidents are most likely to use the veto when the president is more conservative than Congress and when party control is split between the executive and the legislature.

### *Nixon*

For Presidents Nixon and Ford, the veto was a key political strategic force in dealing with Congress (Wayne, 1978: 159). Nixon used the veto rarely in his first three years in office, as his administration realized the negative consequences of veto use. This pattern changed in 1972, when he vetoed seventeen bills in six months. The reason for the change was attributed to Nixon's sense that a broad attack on congressional spending had to be launched, given a failure of congressional compromise by this point (Light, 1982: 112). Though the flood of vetoes did not begin until 1972, the Nixon administration was clearly prepared for this greater veto use. In 1970, the OMB set up a 'legislative watchlist,' whereby staff analysts tracked bills to identify those that might be candidates for veto (this was part of the larger process of 'central clearance' performed by the OMB). Any bill violating the presidential budget or legislative program was placed on the list, which was then passed on to the White House and appropriate departments. This process was continued and expanded under Ford and remained, though less importantly, under Carter (Light, 1982: 115n.).

Nixon's aides were acutely aware of the positive and negative qualities of the veto. Though it was invoked at least partly because of rising concern about federal spending (Light, 1982: 115), the veto had an appeal described by a Nixon aide this way: "It is much easier to turn to the veto. You don't have to devote too much energy over too long a time. At the most, the battle will last two weeks" (Light, 1982: 114). The politics of building a one-third-plus-one coalition continues to make the veto an alluring alternative. On the other hand, the Nixon administration understood the perception that "vetoes were a substitute for legislative compromise, a last resort in congressional stalemate" (Light, 1982: 113).

### *Ford*

Though the veto played an important role in the Nixon administration, his veto use cannot be considered exceptional, given a Congress controlled by the opposing party. In the two-and-one-half year Ford presidency, however, we have a unique case, insofar as Ford was the only twentieth century president to design and pursue a calculated veto strategy. Ford aides commented later that they felt with reluctance that they had no choice but to make the veto the linchpin of their dealings with Congress (Light, 1982: 113–15). This was true because: (1) Ford possessed no congressional base of support, especially after the 1974 midterm elections, when the Watergate backlash brought in forty more Democrats; (2) Ford's approval rating dropped thirty percent from August to October, 1974, in large part because of his pardon of Nixon; (3) the veto was viewed as the best way to demonstrate Ford's commitment to limited government, considered especially important because of Ronald Reagan's challenge from the right in 1976; (4) the Ford people had little or no chance to construct and present a full legislative program of their own, especially since the first priority was to rebuild the presidency itself in the aftermath of Watergate; (5) there was greater concern with fiscal restraint as a primary policy goal, and the veto fit this goal well (as it had for some nineteenth century presidents); and (6) Ford lacked any kind of electoral mandate of his own, further limiting the legitimacy any president needs to promote his objectives.[2]

The short-term benefits of reliance on the veto were clearly understood by the Ford staff, as were the long-term costs. In the long run, Ford's veto use "decreased his opportunities and alienated potential members of the legislative coalition." One Ford aide summarized the drawbacks of the veto strategy this way: "Each veto crippled future opportunities for success; each veto eroded the President's already limited base of support. No President can afford to veto twenty-five bills a year, not in the 1970s at least. It's too damn much, and Congress won't stand for it" (Light, 1982: 111–12). Another Ford aide attributed their loss of Ford's energy package to congressional petulence over frequent veto use. As the aide said, "Why should they [Congress] have listened to us after sixty vetoes?" (Light, 1982: 114). One evidence of mounting congressional frustration was seen in a proposal by New York Democratic Congressman Jonathan Bingham that a veto override for unelected or appointed presidents be reduced to three-fifths (Pessen, 1975).

One consequence of the veto strategy was progressively greater difficulty in sustaining vetoes in Congress. Of sixty-six vetoes in two-and-one-half years, fifty-four were sustained. Of this record, a Ford aide said "Do you know how difficult that was? . . . We had to build a new bloc on each item. We were damn proud of the success" (Light, 1982: 112).

The costs of the veto strategy were felt another way as well. Ford's people felt that, even with an electoral victory establishing a Ford mandate in 1976, he would have been in an exceptionally weak position with respect to Congress. As one aide said of a post-1976 Ford presidency, "Congress wouldn't have listened to Ford. The constant flood of vetoes had angered too many potential allies" (Light, 1982: 113). Again and again, the lack of a positive program was cited as a key problem attendant to the veto strategy. Unlike the Nixon administration, the Ford administration was unable to counterbalance the negative quality of the veto with either parsimony of use or positive alternatives to soften the vetoes and pave the way for future compromises. This sense of Ford administration negativity affected the presidential campaign as well. Though Ford's use of the veto to hold the line on spending met with much popular approval, it also fostered the view that "government by veto was essentially negative government" (Witcover, 1977: 55). This negative image was hardly considered an attractive campaign posture in the 1976 elections.

This vignette of the Ford years parallels that of past veto-prone presidents, especially those who ascended to the presidency through succession rather than election—notably Tyler, Andrew Johnson, and Arthur. The institution of the presidency during Tyler's term, for example, was very different from that of Ford. Yet the consequences of the veto were essentially the same.

### *Carter*

The return of a Democrat saw a return to veto use on a par with that of the Kennedy-Johnson years (Carter vetoed a total of thirty-one bills). Despite Carter's reputed difficulties with Congress (Neustadt, 1980: 210–12), he found relatively little need to resort to the veto. The reason can be seen quite simply in a key contrast between Carter and Ford. Though both presidencies have been viewed as relative failures (as seen notably by the inability of either to be reelected), Ford found himself on the defensive, fighting congressional programs he considered extravagant or unnecessary. As previously mentioned, Ford's administration found itself severely handicapped by its inability to offer a positive program of its own. Carter's situation in this respect was just the reverse. As Neustadt (1980: 215) observes, "Carter suffered from the very scale, diversity, complexity of his initial legislative program." Ford proposed too little, Carter too much. Carter's legislative failing was the inability to realize enactment of enough of his program, which helped to foster an image of Carter as a weak, ineffective president. This was a problem, but it was different from that of Ford, and it was not one that could be resolved by turning to the veto as a major weapon. The last thing Carter needed was to take action which would only fan Congress's already considerable resentment toward this Georgia peanut farmer.

### *Reagan*

The administration of Ronald Reagan has provided a clearcut case of how enduring constitutional issues can reemerge in the midst of contemporary controversy. In the case of the veto power, Reagan's expansive use of the pocket veto (see chapter 4) and his advocacy of item veto power for the president (see chapter 5) have fired longstanding arguments about both. In the case of Reagan's use of the regular veto, an unusual, if telling debate has arisen.

It begins with the perception of Reagan as singularly successful in his dealings with Congress, despite the fact that partisan control of Congress was divided between a Republican Senate and Democratic House in his first six years in office, and under complete Democratic control in 1987 and 1988. The phrase 'Reagan Revolution' has become a euphemism for Reagan's ability, based on enduring personal popularity, generally favorable economic conditions, and adroit politicking, to mold and shape major shifts in national policy (for example, vastly increased defense spending, cuts in many domestic social programs, and a major tax cut). Thus, though Reagan faced a half-hostile (in partisan terms, at least) Congress in his first six years, he scored major policy successes that earned respect from friends and foes alike. Given these circumstances, one would expect minimal veto use. Such has, in fact, been the case. In his first seven years, Reagan vetoed 62 bills (39 in his first four years). Of these 62, eight have been spending bills, and two have involved regular appropriations bills (Rothman, 1984: 2956; update by author). The veto cannot be considered a major tool in Reagan's arsenal in dealing with Congress. Yet Reagan has taken heavy criticism, especially from the right wing of his own party and the business community, for not using the veto vigorously to hold down federal spending levels.

For example, a commentary in *Business Week* (Wildstrom, 1984: 24) rejected Reagan's proposal that he be granted item veto powers as a necessary means of stemming the federal deficit, charging instead that Reagan's existing veto powers were more than adequate for cutting federal spending. The problem was not a lack of power, but a "failure of will." After bemoaning the continued high level of governmental spending and the growing federal deficit, a Prudential-Bache newsletter (1984: 1–2) noted with some disdain that the "word from the White House is that the President will sign just about anything Congress sends him—as long as defense is not hit too hard." An opinion piece on the editorial page of the *Wall Street Journal* (Burton: 1984) concluded that "Mr. Reagan has utterly failed to use what could be his most formidable weapon in reducing federal spending." An article in a publication of the National Taxpayers Union (Haan, 1984) echoed these sentiments: "Mr. Reagan should use the veto as a powerful economic tool, if he wants to ensure that federal spending is brought under control."

A publication produced by the conservative Heritage Foundation (Gattuso and Moore, 1985) accused the president of being "very timid in playing this trump [the veto]." It went on to point out that government spending had actually accelerated under Reagan, as compared with Carter, and that Reagan had failed to kill programs he had initially marked for extinction, such as Amtrak, the Job Corps, the Small Business Administration, Export-Import Bank direct loans, milk and tobacco subsidies, vocational education, and community services block grants. Although Reagan fought most of these bills in Congress, he declined to veto them once they reached his desk.

Another voice from the orthodox economic community promoting a similar message came from the staid *Quality of Earnings Report,* authored by Thornton L. O'glove (1984: 175–78). Though the *Report* focuses principally on analysis of corporate financial statements, some of its pages are devoted to political subjects, including an exhortation that urged Reagan to use the veto to block excess spending. In another publication, the verdict of O'glove and Sobel (1985) was that the "man who has said the two 20th-century presidents he most admires are Franklin Roosevelt and Calvin Coolidge has managed to give us a bit of both—the rhetoric is that of Coolidge the Penurious, but the record more resembles that of FDR the Spender."

A Republican congressman from California, Robert K. Dornan, played loudly to this theme when he issued a press release on July 30, 1985, with the names of 147 members of the House (more than one-third of the chamber) who would sustain any presidential veto involving a bill exceeding Reagan's budget request. Dornan urged the president to adopt an explicit veto strategy to hold down federal spending.

In all of these examples, the concern focuses on the veto as a remedy for the blossoming federal debt, which indeed had doubled in Reagan's first term. These sentiments were also shared by some members of the White House staff, including former Budget Director David Stockman. In his book, Stockman (1986: 157, 234, 336–37, 371–72) described several instances where he and others had urged the issuance of vetoes and/or veto threats against bills that either contradicted the president's agenda, or were "budget-busters." In every instance cited, Reagan backed away from the veto advice. The principal concern on the part of key Reagan advisors such as James Baker, Richard Darman, Edwin Meese, and Donald Regan was to avoid pushing Congress beyond the point at which it would continue to compromise and deal with the White House. Given the significant successes stemming from this restrained political approach, veto restraint was a prudent political move. Here again, too, we see political operatives keenly aware of the substantial costs associated with a true veto strategy. As presidential spokesman Marlin Fitzwater observed, "The less we have to use the veto the better" (*New York Times,* April 4, 1987).

Yet, politics aside, another explanation has been promoted for Reagan's conservative use of the veto to stem spending: The existing veto power is not useful as a means of paring spending, primarily because Congress can attach excess spending measures such as riders onto other, necessary bills. The president is then forced to make a Hobson's choice of approving all or vetoing all. This is precisely the argument Reagan made in his State of the Union Addresses in 1984 and 1985. Reagan's defenders have echoed similar sentiments (e.g. Best, 1984, 1986).

To resolve the question of whether the existing veto power is an adequate device to control spending, one must first acknowledge the obvious. Modern presidents, whether strong or weak by reputation, have enormous authority over every phase of the spending process (e.g. see Fisher, 1975; LeLoup, 1980). The veto may or may not be significant in regulating spending, but to focus on this particular phase of the legislative process at the key to controlling the budget reflects, at best, naïveté about the executive branch's control over bill drafting, central clearance, budgetary coordination by the Office of Management and Budget, executive establishment of budgetary priorities presented to Congress, executive influence over the congressional budget process, and control over spending patterns after bill enactment. In the case of Reagan's conservative critics, the vital fact is that the ballooning deficits of the 1980s, so worrisome to most traditional conservatives, represented the realization, not the frustration, of Reagan's basic agenda, even though they contradicted his oft-stated campaign promise in 1980 to bring down the deficit. The deficits were the inevitable consequence of Reagan's supply-side economics approach. (The underlying assumption of this approach is that if taxes are cut, the revenue saved by the private sector eventually results in more prosperity and, ultimately, more governmental revenue.) Whatever the long-term consequences of this strategy, the short-term consequence has been a decrease in federal revenue coupled with vastly increased defense spending and cuts in other spending areas insufficient to close the yawning deficit gap (O'glove and Sobel, 1985). According to David Stockman (1986), the great failing of the Reagan administration has been its unwillingness to cut meaningfully into entrenched spending patterns despite past tough rhetoric. Indeed, the rate of governmental spending, controlling for inflation, has increased since 1980, compared to the Carter years (see *New York Times,* February 2, 1986).

To return to the role of the veto, two issues arise concerning its efficacy against excess spending: (1) whether it has been used successfully in the past by other presidents to excise undesirable riders from necessary legislation; and (2) the fiscal consequences of vetoes by other presidents. The first of these two questions was addressed extensively in chapter 2. Without question, presidents have resented the uncomfortable situation of being presented with legislation containing undesired riders or other amendments. Yet presidents who have faced this dilemma by making the decision to veto, such as Hayes, Cleveland, Taft, Wilson, and both Roosevelts, have usually found success in forcing the hand of Congress. Bejamin Harrison's (1897: 132) philosophy about riders was that "many laws contain more than one proposition . . . and the President must deal with them as thus associated." Even Washington's two vetoes caused Congress to excise or alter objectionable portions of vetoed bills. Clearly, a president who relies overly much on the veto for this or any purpose risks fanning the flames of congressional resentment against him. But the records of most presidents make clear that the presidents' preferences invariably weigh heavily on the minds of congressmen. As long as America maintains a system of checks and balances, two facts will persist: (1) The veto will remain a viable tool for weeding out riders (including those that are responsible for excess spending); and (2) the veto will never unfailingly prevent periodic successful attachment of special spending provisions and other riders to legislation. The day Congress is unable to enact such attachments, with at least some success, is the day presidents will no longer need Congress to enact legislation.

As to the second question of the relative success of other presidents in using the veto to hold down spending, a comparison can be made between Reagan's record and that of his recent predecessors. One of the first and most frequently cited rationales for vetoes has been the presidential aim of holding down spending. Though this presidential claim often masks more pedantic political concerns, there is certainly nothing new about this justification for the veto (see chapter 5). Yet concern about size of the budget and the federal deficit has emerged with new force as a political issue in the aftermath of the free-spending era of the 1960s. This held true especially during the Ford, Carter, and Reagan presidencies. More than their recent predecessors, these three presidents elevated the budget-cutting limited government theme by emphasizing it as both an election issue and a major policy goal. To use Ford and Carter as standards of comparison, how did their veto use compare with that of Reagan in terms of its impact on spending?

To answer this question, I examined bills vetoed by presidents to determine what programs, and therefore what spending, were successfully blocked. Each bill vetoed by Ford, Carter, and Reagan (through 1986) was examined to determine the level of spending that would have resulted had the bill been enacted. This figure was derived from the bill itself, or estimates offered by the Congressional Budget Office, the OMB, congressmen, or the president (in the case of contradictory assessments, a compromise figure was selected).[3] Both authorization and appropriation figures were included in spending totals (understanding that an authorization is the granting of the right to spend money, whereas an appropriation actually allocates money for a specific purpose), but both figures were not counted for the same particular bills. In those few instances where the president vetoed the authorization but approved the appropriation (as Reagan did in his vetoes of a Federal Maritime Commission authorization bill on

October 28, and a NASA authorization bill on November 14, 1986), the dollar figure for the authorization was not included in the total dollar amount vetoed. When the president's veto of a bill involving spending was overridden, the spending was not included in the president's budget-cutting total since the principal concern here is with presidential success, not presidential intent.[4] Also, a sustained veto often prompts Congress to come back with the same bill later, but accounting for the president's spending or other objections. The fate of vetoed bills was traced for just this eventuality. Thus, if the president vetoed a $10 billion appropriations bill and the veto was sustained, but the Congress later approved an $8 billion appropriation for the same purpose and the president then signed the bill, he would be given credit for a $2 billion savings.

In President Ford's two-and-one-half years in office, he vetoed bills resulting in savings of $41 billion (this and all figures adjusted for inflation). In Carter's four years, presidential vetoes resulted in $24 billion in spending cuts. In Reagan's first six years, his vetoes resulted in savings of $15 billion. When yearly averages are computed, Ford leads the way with $16.4 billion, followed by Carter with $6 billion, and then Reagan with $2.5 billion.[5] There can be no doubt that Reagan's recent predecessors succeeded far more than he in employing the veto to help achieve fiscal economy. Reagan's failure to apply the veto in a similar fashion stems not from any shortcoming of the veto power itself (Reagan's average number of vetoes per year is 9.1 for his first six years, actually greater than Carter's yearly average of 7.7), but rather from differing policy decisions about what and what not to veto. Reagan's relatively low veto average may be taken as a sign of his success in getting policy concessions without resort to the veto; yet, this leads us again to the inescapable conclusion that Reagan's complaints about a spendthrift Congress and oversized deficit mask the fact that overall spending patterns during his administration are the logical consequence of the realization of his own programs and goals. This conclusion is offered despite the escalation of Reagan's budget-cutting rhetoric after the 1984 election. Reagan even borrowed a line from a popular movie by daring Congress to exceed his recommended spending levels, promising a veto with the phrase, "Go ahead and make my day" (*New York Times,* March 14, 1985).

Although President Reagan did not use the veto to "make his day" in a budgetary sense, the veto was the focal point of several major policy controversies between the two branches of government, especially during the ninety-ninth Congress. Two of these controversies are discussed here. Both cases are atypical in that a strong president suffered the defeat of a successful veto override and a near defeat in an area where presidents dominate—foreign affairs. Moreover, these setbacks occurred during a period when the president's party controlled the Senate. Nevertheless, both cases are instructive.

## Two cases

### *The Saudi arms deal*[6]

One overt sign of presidential dominance in foreign affairs is that no president has ever had a proposed arms sale turned down by Congress. At the same time, however, presidents have withdrawn or modified arms requests to sway members of Congress and avoid political embarassment. Such was the case of Reagan's 1986 proposal to sell missiles to Saudi Arabia. The proposed $354 million package included 100 air-to-sea Harpoons, 1666 air-to-air Sidewinders, and 200 ground-to-air, shoulder-held Stingers (with 600 reload missiles). Part of the bargaining behind this bill was based on the fact that informal but overwhelming Senate opposition had forced the cancellation of a billion-dollar package, planned for the Saudis in 1985, which included F–15 jet fighters, M–1 tanks, helicopter gunships, and other auxiliary equipment. Congressional resistance to the scaled-down arms proposal was nevertheless stiff from the outset because of resentment over Saudi Arabia's support for the Palestine Liberation Organization and Syria, refusal to support Egypt and Jordan in the peace process, and continued belligerence toward Israel (*New York Times,* March 1, 1986).

Congress had fifty days to attempt to block the arms sale. On May 6, the Republican-controlled Senate voted to disapprove the arms sale, 73–22 (SJ Res 316). The following day, the Democratic House did the same by a vote of 356–62 (HJ Res 589). On May 21, Reagan vetoed the disapproval, setting up the pivotal conflict over the proposed arms sale.[7] The relative ease and lopsided margin of congressional disapproval occurred, partly because Israeli lobbying forces dropped their opposition to the deal, wishing to conserve their political resources for political battles in which the threat to Israel was greater. Israeli representatives suggested that the scaled-down arms package did not pose a major threat, as Saudi Arabia already owned the missiles included in the package ("Pro-Israel Lobby Declines to Fight Arms Sale," 1986: 703). In addition, the Reagan administration did little to stave off early opposition in Congress. Much to the dismay of pro-Arab groups and defense contractors, little effort was made to try and block the disapproval vote before it reached Reagan's desk. Whatever its wisdom, the administration clearly pursued a veto strategy by deciding to focus most of its energies on sustaining Reagan's May 21 veto ("Proposed Saudi Missile Sale Gathers Opposition on Hill," 1986: 916; "Congress Shoots Down a Saudi Missile Sale," 1986). In the words of administration supporter and Republican Congressman Henry J. Hyde, "I would not say that the president put on a full-court press or a half-court press or even a quarter-court press" ("Both Chambers Say 'No' to Saudi Arms Deal," 1986: 1020). Aside from the apparent ease of a veto strategy, White House aides were partially lulled by Israel's lack of concern about the sale and so concentrated their attention on other issues deemed more pressing.

The administration focused its resources on the vote in the Senate to override the veto. Reagan critics continued to voice concern about the use of arms sales as a primary means of diplomacy and were particularly concerned about the inclusion of shoulder-held Stinger missiles in the package. Persistent concerns were expressed that, given the volatility of the Middle East, such weapons could find their way into the hands of terrorists. (The potent, 35-pound Stinger is considered a 'terrorist's delight.')

The administration marshalled support for sustaining the veto in two ways. First, it continued to promote the argument that Saudi Arabia was a friend of the U.S. as a supplier of oil and as a moderate voice in the Arab world. Along these lines, Reagan noted with some alarm the need to counter both Soviet and Iranian influence in the Middle East. Second, the administration removed the Stinger missiles from the package, reducing the total price tag to $265 million. Reagan indicated his intention to omit the Stingers in a letter to Senate Majority Leader Robert Dole, delivered on the day of the veto. Though the administration claimed that the change occurred at the behest of the Saudis, Saudi leaders made clear their displeasure (*New York Times,* May 21, 1986). The excision was also a clear symptom of the administration's almost frenzied effort to salvage the deal in this final stage.

Pressure on the Senate focused on winning over at least twelve votes to provide the minimum thirty-four-vote margin needed to sustain the veto. Reagan campaigned personally, calling more than dozen senators. An added bonus came from former President Jimmy Carter, who contacted several Democrats, urging them to support the sale. The effectiveness of this pressure stemmed partly from a key, recurring argument: The president's ability to provide foreign policy leadership could be impaired if his preferences were openly denied by the Congress. One opponent of the sale who switched his vote on the override was Republican Senator John P. East, who explained his switch by saying that "the president should be allowed to make foreign policy without being managed at every turn by the Congress" (*New York Times,* June 6, 1986).

On June 5, the Senate voted to sustain the veto by a 34–66 vote—the exact vote needed to prevent an override. That the politics of this arms package reflected confusion and backpeddling was reflected in *Time* magazine's stinging, if exaggerated comment that this was "one of the sorriest foreign policy messes on record" ("No-Win Battle over Saudi Arms," 1986: 19).

### *South African sanctions*

In 1986, an increase in American outrage at actions of the South African government converged with deteriorating political conditions in that nation. The convergence produced a significant symbolic setback for the white minority government there and for the Reagan administration. As the cycle of violence escalated in South Africa in the spring of 1986, highlighted by South African bombing raids and commando attacks on suspected guerrilla camps in neighboring countries as well as increased repression within South Africa's borders, congressional leaders moved to impose new, tougher sanctions. It did so despite the persistent opposition of the Reagan administration, which since 1981 had pursued a policy of 'constructive engagement,' which emphasized low-key persuasion aimed at South Africa's leaders and designed to encourage a voluntary end to the white minority's long-standing policy of racial apartheid. House Democratic critic Stephen Solarz echoed the opinion of many in Congress when he concluded that "the [Reagan] policy has failed" ("House Panels Prepare the Way for South African Sanctions Bill," 1986: 1318).

In its initial form, the sanctions bill (considered first in the House) would have barred new American investments in and loans to South Africa and would have both cut off imports of South African uranium, coal, and steel and ended U.S. involvement in energy development and computer assistance. But in an apparently surprise move, this sanctions bill was displaced by a tougher measure invoking a complete trade embargo on the country requiring all American companies to leave South Africa within 180 days. The latter measure, passed by voice vote (HR 4868), was sponsored by Democratic Congressman Ronald Dellums. The ease of passage of this bill partly reflected a Republican recognition that a tougher House bill would have a more difficult time in the Senate ("Stunner in House," 1986: 1384).

Most Reagan administration efforts to block a sanctions bill were directed at the Republican-controlled Senate. Reagan hoped to stave off a sanctions bill there by following his strategy of the previous year of enacting a few sanction measures through executive order, and in doing so "calculating the minimum changes . . . needed to stall the Senate's rush to sanctions" ("Reagan Is Seeking to Head Off Senate Action on South Africa," 1986: 1606). But, unlike their response in 1985, key Senate Republicans openly challenged Reagan's approach. Leading the charge was Republican Foreign Relations Committee Chairman Richard Lugar and Subcommittee on African Affairs Chairman Nancy Kassebaum. The rift between the Senate and the president widened with the spread of South African repression during the summer and Reagan's continued defense of friendly persuasion ("Administration's Role: How Much Is Enough?" 1986: 1386). Though Reagan dropped the term 'constructive engagement,' he continued to praise the Pretoria government's "dramatic change" in addressing the apartheid problem ("Pressure Builds for New South Africa Sanctions," 1986: 1672).

With Lugar's guidance and Democratic support, the Senate produced a sanctions bill (S.2701) similar to that of the original House bill. It included barring South African Airways from American skies and banned importation of steel, coal, uranium, and agricultural products. It also barred new American investment in South Africa and threatened further sanctions if no improvements in apartheid were forthcoming. After two days of intense debate, the Senate adopted the Lugar bill 84–14 on August 15. Lugar then succeeded in pressing the House to accept the Senate version rather than risk delay and stalemate in a conference committee. By a 308–70 vote, the House approved the Senate version on September 12. The Reagan administration continued to express misgivings about the sanctions, fearing that the measure would have a "negative effect" on the region and "would impede, rather than advance, our goals of promoting further change in South Africa" (*New York Times,* September 13, 1986).

Though the bill was more important for its symbolic than its substantive consequences, it was a resounding rejection of the Reagan approach. The break between the president and Congress was exacerbated not only by Reagan's reluctance to compromise but also by his slow and tardy political response. For example, Reagan did not, as expected, accompany his September 26 veto with an executive order imposing his own sanctions. Rather, he only hinted at possible tough measures despite the verdict that a veto override "would represent an unprecedented congressional rebuff of Reagan on a major foreign policy issue" ("Bucking Strong Hill Sentiment, Reagan Vetoes South Africa Bill," 1986: 2268). A few days after the veto, Reagan announced the impending appointment of a black to serve as ambassador to South Africa and also voiced a request for new economic aid for the black nations of southern Africa. But these moves did little to assuage criticism.

Three days after the veto, the House voted to override, 313–83. No administration attempt was made to alter the House vote. In the Senate, Reagan efforts were "limited." According to one assessment, "the administration never pulled out all the stops to support the veto in the Senate" ("Hill Overrides Veto of South Africa Sanctions," 1986: 2339). The relative absence of Reagan leadership was summarized by Republican Senator John H. Chafee who noted: "You don't like seeing a President's veto overridden, and it's unfortunate that it's come to this. Had the President jumped in earlier, he could have guided this debate" (*New York Times,* October 3, 1986). Although Reagan picked up seven votes through personal intervention, the Senate easily overrode the veto on October 2, 78–21. Given Reagan's unwillingness to compromise, one observer concluded that the vote was not a winnable one for the president. Even Senate

Republican leaders lent only half-hearted support to Reagan. These considerations notwithstanding, enactment of the sanctions (PL99–440) was considered "the most serious defeat Reagan has suffered on a foreign issue and one of the most stunning blows of his presidency" and was compared to the 1973 enactment of the War Powers Resolution over President Nixon's veto ("Hill Overrides Veto of South Africa Sanctions," 1986: 2338). With an election approaching and public opinion clearly in their favor, members of Congress felt emboldened to challenge the president. The Reagan administration, in turn, took few effective actions to stem the congressional tide.

These two brief cases underscore several important observations. First, the appearance of defeat on a veto is more worrisome for the president than the reality of defeat. In the case of the Saudi arms sale, the two-thirds reduction in size of the arms package meant far less in a political sense than the ability of the president to make *some* kind of sale. Similarly, the imposition of presidentially originated sanctions against South Africa, though provoked solely by the desire to avoid a veto override in 1985, was viewed as a face-saving action by the president. The fact that Reagan did not move more quickly and decisively to do so in 1986 egged on his opponents, yielding a politically embarassing override—though the loss was not of the same order as Nixon's defeat on the War Powers Resolution issue.

Second, in both veto cases, feelings of ambivalence and reluctance surrounded the challenge to the two vetoes. Though staunch Reagan adversaries no doubt felt some glee, Republican defectors and others expressed mixed feelings about challenging the president, especially in foreign affairs. Also, some sided with the president solely because of the sense that the president had the right to conduct foreign policy without congressional meddling.

Third, in neither case did the president "pull out all the stops." Given Reagan's undisputed record of adroit politicking, one must assume that the Reagan people could have fought harder, and with greater effect, in both cases. No doubt they would have done so had the two issues been more pressing for the White House. The veto strategy in the Saudi arms case was a consciously minimal strategy that succeeded by a single vote. The sanctions defeat was handled with less skill, reflecting an apparently inexorable clash involving Reagan's refusal to abandon the substance of constructive engagement, the issue's relatively low priority in the White House, and the lack of support in Congress and the country for any such accommodation of South Africa. This wedge between Reagan and the Congress is not surprising given the fact that Reagan was in the sixth year of his presidency and the tendency for veto use and veto challenges to become more likely as a presidency wears on.[8] Moreover, the veto as appeal to the public is a key to its potency, and in neither case was Congress bucking public opinion. These observations lead us to a final, underappreciated quality of the veto power.

## The veto threat

This important and usually underrated quality of the veto power warrants separate mention. The power of a presidential veto threat was recognized even before the Constitution was adopted. In Federalist #73 (1961: 446) Alexander Hamilton took special note of this consequence of the veto power.

> A power of this nature in the executive will often have a silent and unperceived, though forcible, operation. When men, engaged in unjustifiable pursuits, are aware that obstructions may come from a quarter which they cannot control, they will often be restrained by the bare apprehension of opposition from doing what they would with eagerness rush into if no such external impediments were to be feared.

Four months into his first term, President Washington expressed his displeasure over a tonnage bill that Congress had just passed. It was too late for Congress to take back or alter the original bill, so in response, Congress passed another bill more to the president's liking. Congress evinced keen interest in Washington's opinions concerning pending legislation on several other occasions as well (Thomson, 1978).

Despite early use of the veto threat and countenance of the threat in the *Federalist Papers,* presidential critics decried its use as inappropriate and even unconstitutional, especially during the Monroe, Jackson, and Tyler presidencies (see chapter 2). Yet even during this period, its legitimacy was recognized. Writing in 1833 (350), Justice

Story observed of the veto that "one of the greatest benefits of such a power is, that its influence is felt, not so much in its actual exercise, as in its silent and secret energy as a preventive. It checks the intention to usurp, before it has ripened into an act." The potency of the threat continued to be recognized (e.g. Beard, 1914: 614; Berdahl, 1937: 510). Writing much more recently, Davidson (1984: 373) noted that "the most potent vetoes are those that are never used but are merely posed as threats."

The veto threat's special value is as a tool to shape, alter, or deter legislation before it reaches the president's desk. Like the veto itself, a threat applied too often loses its potency, and a threat not thought of as credible is not a threat at all. For modern presidents, however, the veto threat is unquestionably a vital aspect of presidential dealings with Congress. Both the Nixon and Ford administrations incorporated the veto threat as an integral part of their legislative strategies. As Wayne (1978: 159) reported: "Liaison aides used the threat of a presidential veto to influence the Democratic majority to tailor its legislative proposals so that they would be acceptable to the president." A legislative coordinator during the Nixon-Ford years estimated that the veto threat resulted in legislative alterations favorable to the president in twenty to thirty cases. Carter applied the threat when, for example, he made public his intention to veto any bill containing tuition tax credits. Carter's announcement prompted Congress to remove such a program from its 1978 education bill despite the fact that the Senate had already given its approval (Tatalovich and Daynes, 1984: 150).

In order to assess in a systematic way the nature and frequency of the use of the veto threat by recent presidents (since Kennedy), the *New York Times Index* was searched from 1961 to 1986 for publically issued or reported veto threats.[9] One cannot assume that all veto threats grabbed significant newspaper attention, but much effort is expended by both Congress and the media to discern the president's opinion on important legislation (and even unimportant bills require presidential approval). It is thus reasonable to assume that most serious veto threats would wind up being reported, and that comparisons between presidents can be readily made. Also, much of the political value of a veto threat is its public nature.

In the aftermath of a veto threat, four possible actions can occur: (1) Congress backs down and the bill dies in Congress after recognition that stated presidential opposition means that further effort on behalf of the bill is no longer fruitful; (2) a compromise can occur between the branches, leading to passage of the modified bill and presidential signature; (3) the president backs down by changing his mind, acceding to congressional preferences; or (4) neither side backs down, Congress passes the bill unchanged, and it is vetoed. The determination of whether a conflict resulted in a congressional victory, a presidential victory, or a compromise was based on evaluations that appeared in the *Times.*

As table 3–4 shows, the veto threat was not employed (at least in any readily visible respect) by Kennedy and Johnson. This is consonant with their rare veto use. Nixon applied the veto threat on 5 occasions noted in *Times* reporting, then found it necessary to actually veto all 5 bills. Ford issued twice the number of threats, forcing Congress to back down on 2 occasions. Carter issued 12 threats. On 8 of these occasions, he either won concessions or Congress backed down. On only 2 occasions did the Democratic-controlled Congress force a veto confrontation. Also on 2 occasions, Carter backed down. Reagan has been by far the most prolific user of the veto threat. He succeeded in either getting Congress to back down or obtaining compromise in 19 instances out of 29 (about the same two-thirds ratio as Carter despite facing a House controlled by the Democrats); yet, Congress has also defied Reagan 9 times. The most important trend to be noted from these data is the general rise in veto threats. Given the desirability of settling disputes before the stage where strategy dictates the issuance of public threats, the rise of such threats can be taken as one more indicator of recent presidential-congressional contentiousness. The rise of veto threats is also seen in per year averages: Nixon averaged .9 per year; Ford 4 per year; Carter 3 per year; and Reagan 4.8 per year.

Of the 56 bills subject to veto threats since 1961, the largest number (19) involved appropriations and spending bills. The next largest number (18) involved specific programs objectionable to the president, such as economic sanctions levied against other countries, public works bills, mass transit, and other, mostly distributive bills. Eleven bills involved regulatory matters, and 8 involved categorical social aid programs. All presidents examined who used the threat did so against appropriations bills in the name of fiscal restraint, but Reagan did this the most. Ford focused most of his threats against

**Table 3–4**
**Fate of Veto-Threatened Bills**

| *President* | *Total threatened bills* | *Congress backs down; bill dies* | *Compromise* | *President backs down; bill enacted* | *Bill passed as is and vetoed* | *Vetoes overridden* |
|---|---|---|---|---|---|---|
| Kennedy | 0 | 0 | 0 | 0 | 0 | 0 |
| Johnson | 0 | 0 | 0 | 0 | 0 | 0 |
| Nixon | 5 | 0 | 0 | 0 | 5 | 1 |
| Ford | 10 | 2 | 0 | 0 | 8 | 1 |
| Carter | 12 | 3 | 5 | 2 | 2 | 1 |
| Reagan (1981–1986) | 29 | 8 | 11 | 1 | 9 | 2 |

Source: *New York Times Annual Index, 1961–1986.* The numbers of veto threats listed above are not considered definitive. Threats may have been delivered by Presidents Kennedy and Johnson, for example, but not have been reported in the newspapers; however, there is no doubt that presidents with larger numbers of threats used them more, as their potency is dependent in large part on the extent to which they are widely known.

specific programs and regulatory bills, evincing a relatively stronger commitment to traditional conservatism.

## Conclusion

Without question, the veto power continues to be potent, effective, important, and temptingly simple to apply though cost-laden if used frequently or injudiciously. These qualities apply just as they did in the nineteenth century. The veto is itself a symptom of partisan and institutional conflict between the legislative and executive branches of government. Though the veto power is unchanged, its handling has become institutionalized and been made routine—along with White House handling of most other important aspects of the legislative process—through central clearance and the enrolled-bill process. The only aspect of the veto process that continues to arouse little interest is the handling of private bills (although this could change in the future).

Most recent presidents have been given brief treatment here since their use of the veto represented nothing new in terms of the power itself. Two recent presidents have, however, been closely enmeshed with important aspects of veto politics. The Ford administration found itself relying on a true veto strategy. The effectiveness of the strategy was seen both in the large number of vetoes sustained and in Ford's defeat in 1976.

The Reagan administration relied on a different kind of veto strategy. Possessing a strong electoral mandate and the ability to keep it for most of the presidency, the Reagan administration had little need for a Ford-like reliance on vetoes. Instead, it relied on veto rhetoric and symbols—tough veto talk, regular use of the veto threat, and persistent advocacy of an item veto power—to advance the president's image and agenda. In this way, Reagan reaped maximum benefits with minimum political cost.

In the panoply of presidential powers, the veto may seem small. But as with the vetoes of past presidents in past eras, the power is central, and reveals much about the institution as a whole.

# 4

# The Pocket Veto

*Antonio: If but one of his pockets could speak, would it not say he lies?*
*Sebastian: Ay, or very falsely pocket up his report.*

William Shakespeare
*The Tempest,* Act II, Scene 1

On November 30, 1983, President Reagan ignited a significant constitutional controversy when he pocket vetoed a bill that linked American aid to the Central American nation of El Salvador with improvement of its record on human rights. The controversy had less to do with continued American support of El Salvador than with the fact that Reagan used the pocket veto between two sessions of the Ninety-eighth Congress.

There is no little irony in the fact that, after the exercise of over a thousand pocket vetoes during a period of over one hundred and eighty years, ambiguity has persisted as to when and under wht circumstances the pocket veto may be properly applied. We will return to the Reagan case later; for the moment, the pocket veto controversy warrants elaboration.

## How the pocket veto works

It is important to understand first that the pocket veto is "in an entirely different category from the ordinary veto" (Zinn, 1951: 29). The relevant sentence in the Constitution (article I, section 7) is deceptively simple: "If any Bill shall not be returned by the President within ten Days (Sundays excepted) after it shall have been presented to him, the Same shall be a Law, in like manner as if he had signed it, unless the Congress by their Adjournment prevent its Return, in which Case it shall not be a Law." The first part of the sentence states that if the president takes no action on bills presented to him they become law automatically after ten days. The necessity of this is evident: Without such a qualification the president could halt bills at any time simply by withholding his signature. This circumstance is modified by the phrase "unless the Congress by their Adjournment prevent its Return," in which case any bill not signed is vetoed, though not returned to Congress for reconsideration. Any such bills are, in effect, absolute-vetoed by the president. Under these circumstances, members of Congress wishing to reconsider a pocket vetoed bill must begin again at the next meeting of Congress by reintroducing the bill.

## What did the founders know, and when did they know it?

The pocket veto power raises an immediate, intriguing question: Did the founders realize the consequences of this sentence? This question acquires greater significance with the realization that the founders considered on several occasions a proposal to grant the president an absolute veto, yet they voted unanimously on each occasion against it despite the prodding of James Wilson and Alexander Hamilton (see chapter 1). An absolute veto resembled too closely the despised veto power of the British monarch. What, then, was the purpose of this absolute veto?

Looking back at the *Records of the Federal Convention,* one finds no debate on the subject. Yet several clues illuminate the mystery. First, the one important difference between the federal veto and that in the New York Constitution of 1777 (after which the federal veto was patterned), is that the latter called for bills vetoed by the governor to be held over until the legislature reconvened. This was changed in the federal Constitution because it was feared that Congress might try to avoid a veto by simply adjourning, thereby preventing timely return of bills to Congress. Without this return, there is no veto. This concern over presidential self-protection was the motivating force behind the pocket veto (Story, 1833, II: 355). In other words, it was conceived as a defense to ensure that the president would not be deprived of the opportunity to disapprove legislation, *not* as an affirmative grant of power to the president (e.g., see *Barnes v. Kline,* 759 F.2d 21 (1985): 38). There is no reason to believe that the founders did not understand the implications of what they were doing.[1] At the same time, it is logical to assume that they would not be sanguine about prolific presidential use of an absolute veto.

## Evolution of the pocket veto

As table 3.1 showed, the pocket veto was used sparingly until after the Civil War (though the same could be said of the regular veto). While some of the circumstances of regular veto use were hotly debated, the power itself was not questioned. The same cannot be said of the pocket veto, however.

The first two pocket vetoes, exercised by President Madison in 1812 and 1816, received relatively little notice and were uncontroversial. The next president to use the pocket veto was Andrew Jackson (the term *pocket veto* was apparently coined by critics during his administration; see Vose [1964]: 398), who applied it in seven of his twelve vetoes. Jackson's critics raged that the express purpose of the pocket veto was to "guard against a sudden adjournment, by which the President might be deprived of due time to deliberate on an important bill." Since the congressional adjournment precipitating the particular pocket vetoes in question was not sudden, Jackson's "withholding the bill was arbitrary and unconstitutional" according to one critic, as "Congress and the Senate . . . were deprived of their constitutional right of passing on the bill, after the President had exercised his powers" (*Debates in Congress,* December 5, 1833: 18).

The aged James Madison, writing to Jackson critic Henry Clay in 1833, voiced similar misgivings about use of the pocket veto. He suggested that applying a pocket veto to a bill "of sufficient magnitude . . . might doubtless be a ground for impeachment." This rather extreme conclusion, coming ironically from the first president to use the pocket veto, was provoked by the importance he attached to two key components of the legislative process: (1) that the president have "adequate time to consider the bills"; and (2) "that Congress should have time to consider and overrule the objections." For either side to interfere with the other would constitute "an abuse for which it would be responsible under the forms of the Constitution" (Watson, 1910, I: 365–66, n.39).

President Buchanan issued a strong defense of the pocket veto's necessity in an 1860 pocket veto memorandum, invoking what was indeed a serious problem attendant to the rush of legislation at the end of a session: "To require him [the president] to approve a bill when it is impossible he could examine into its merits would be to deprive him of the exercise of his constitutional discretion and convert him into a mere register of the decrees of Congress" (*Messages,* 1913, IV: 3130–31).

Criticism of the pocket veto persisted. An essay which otherwise defended the veto power said of the pocket veto that it was "a kind of bastard veto . . . which is plainly an abuse, unauthorized by the Constitution, and an invasion of the rights of the people and of their representatives" (Long, 1887: 260–61). Long's specific objection was not to use of the pocket veto by a president swamped with end-of-session legislation but to use by a president who simply decided to rely on the pocket veto because a bill reached his desk within ten days of congressional adjournment. Though this complaint merits some attention, the Constitution makes no allowance for the intent behind veto use (as Long also noted).

## Persisting pocket veto ambiguities

Although the pocket veto power itself is now unequivocally accepted (its use escalated along with that of the regular veto), several questions related to its use remain. One key question is that of adjournment. Given that the Constitution allows for a pocket veto after congressional adjournment, what exactly constitutes an adjournment? Also, may the president approve bills after Congress has adjourned? May representatives of Congress and the president serve as legal stand-ins to, for example, receive enrolled bills and veto messages? Presidents are obliged to provide written messages of explanation for regular vetoes, but are they obliged to do the same for pocket vetoes? Is two-thirds of a quorum, as opposed to two-thirds of all members, all that is required for a successful veto override? Some of these questions have been resolved by court rulings.

### *Court cases and the veto power*

A handful of Supreme Court rulings have addressed ambiguities concerning the veto power, generally pertaining to the veto around adjournment time. The first case was that of *La Abra Silver Mining Co. v. U.S.* (175 U.S. 423), rendered in 1899. The case involved the question of whether a bill, duly passed by Congress but signed into law by the president after Congress had recessed (to reconvene at a later set date), was in fact a law, given that the signing occurred after Congress was no longer in session. Speaking for the Court, Justice Harlan argued that such an approval was legal since it occurred within the ten-day period. The court rejected the contention that the president could not sign bills when Congress was not in session despite the court's recognition that the president was participating in a legislative act. The matter of signing bills after an adjournment is pertinent to this discussion for two reasons: First, the prevailing sentiment (and practice) up to this time was that the president did not have this power (e.g., Renick, 1898; Rogers, 1920); and second, to be able to sign bills after adjournment (now the accepted practice) helped buttress the pocket veto power, since such bills would be automatically vetoed if they were not given the presidential signature. Presidents avoided these problems for the first 150 years of the country's history by traveling to the Capitol on the last day of a congressional session to sign those bills that were not to be vetoed (Zinn, 1951: 19). The very fact that this practice was the norm is a clear indication that the founders placed great store in allowing Congress every opportunity to react to final presidential actions, including vetoes, before concluding its business (Renick, 1898: 13).

An unusual case illustrating this relationship arose in 1824. By accident, President Monroe had omitted his signature from one out of about fifty bills passed and signed on the last day of the congressional session. Monroe called his cabinet together to discuss the problem. Attorney General Wirt suggested that the bill might be simply signed and back-dated. Secretary of State John Quincy Adams suggested that there was no prohibition preventing the president from signing the bill after adjournment. Secretary of War Calhoun dissented from both propositions. Monroe decided that the bill could not be considered a law, fearing "misapprehensions of [the president's] motives" (Renick, 1898: 209). President Lincoln finally set the precedent of signing a bill after Congress had adjourned in 1863, though Congress later objected and repassed the bill the following session.

President Grant offered his own remedy by proposing a constitutional amendment forbidding Congress from passing any laws—except by overriding vetoes—during the final twenty-four hours of its session to provide the president with greater opportunity to examine them (Harrison, 1897: 131). President Cleveland became the first president to refuse to travel to the Capitol during the final days of the congressional session.

The next Supreme Court case involving the veto was *Missouri Pacific Railway Co. v. Kansas* (248 U.S. 276), rendered in 1919. It resolved a question that Congress had dealt with for itself the previous century—namely, what voting majority was necessary to meet the two-thirds veto override requirement. Citing past congressional practice and the existing requirements for conducting other business (including constitutional amendments), the court upheld the decision that two-thirds of a quorum, rather than two-thirds of all members, is acceptable for a successful veto override. Though not directly pertinent to the pocket veto, the ruling amicably resolved a lingering ambiguity.

The next case, also the most well known, is *The Pocket Veto Case* (1929; 279 U.S. 644).[2] The case came about as the result of a challenge of a pocket veto by President Coolidge. The veto occurred at the end of the first session of Congress, at the start of an adjournment running from July to December, 1926. Speaking for the court, Justice Sanford noted first that the specific question was whether the congressional adjournment had prevented the president from returning the bill in question (an Indian tribes claim bill) to Congress within ten days. The court noted the time problem faced by the president, given the importance of his final deliberations "for adequately formulating the objections that should be considered by Congress" (678). It flatly rejected the contention that the ten-day period for presidential consideration of bills count as ten legislative days (that is, days when Congress is in session), favoring the interpretation of the words "in their natural and obvious sense" (679) as meaning ten calendar days (except Sundays). The Court then grappled with the key question of the meaning of "adjournment," noting that "the determinative question in reference to an 'adjournment' is not whether it is a final adjournment of Congress or an interim adjournment . . . but whether it is one that 'prevents' the President from returning the bill to the House in which it originated within the time allowed" (680). They rejected the idea that a bill could be returned, even to a duly authorized agent, when Congress was not literally convened and in session. The court also noted, however, that Congress had never formally designated any officer or agent to receive returned bills during adjournment. Their objection to this return of a bill was founded not only on the fact that Congress had never given such an authorization to an agent, but also that such a return might leave a bill "in a state of suspended animation. . . . for days, weeks, or perhaps months" (684). Timely return of a bill was of great importance, as was prompt congressional reconsideration. Finally, the court also noted that, up to this time, available data revealed 119 instances, out of over 400 past pocket vetoes, of such vetoes occurring between sessions of Congress (the rest occurred at the ends of Congresses).[3] To underscore what is perhaps the pivotal point, the decision noted that the key question was the ability of the president to return the bill, *not* the definition of adjournment (though a more precise definition might help resolve ambiguity). Although it rejected the idea of an agent acting on behalf of Congress, the court also seemed to outline a strategy whereby this problem might be overcome. These issues were picked up again in a 1938 case.

Three years later, the court extended its ruling in the *La Abra* case by ruling that the president could sign a bill into law not only when Congress had recessed to reconvene at a set date, but also after Congress had adjourned *sine die* (*Edwards v. U.S.* (1932) [286 U.S. 482]). Once again, the court emphasized two vital interests: that Congress have the opportunity for prompt reconsideration of bills; and that the president have the opportunity to properly consider all bills before him. The court also noted that the veto power is a legislative power.

The fifth case raising veto issues was *Wright v. U.S.* (1938) (302 U.S. 583), and it involved a regular veto of a bill that was returned to the secretary of the Senate during a three-day Senate recess. Writing for the court, Chief Justice Hughes noted that the recess in question was not "an adjournment" (the House was still in session). More pertinent to the *Pocket Veto* case, the court contradicted its previous assertion by saying now that the "Constitution does not define what shall constitute a return of a bill or deny the use of appropriate agencies in effecting the return" (589). The court saw no problem with the use of duly designated messengers for each branch of government, rejecting the notion of any "artificial formality" (590). It also dismissed the delay problem attributed to the use of agents mentioned in the *Pocket Veto* case as being, in this instance, "illusory" (595). The court decision cited at some length the amicus curiae brief of the losing side of the *Pocket Veto* case to buttress this point. In a concurring opinion, Justice Stone, joined by Justice Brandeis, emphasized even more strongly that Congress could legally designate agents to receive returned bills. He went on to discuss the *Pocket Veto* case, concluding that "it should now be frankly overruled" (604). Stone concluded by emphasizing adjournment "as that which prevents return" (608). Thus, any action facilitating the return of vetoed bills, including the designation of agents when Congress is not in session, is in keeping with the meaning and spirit of the Constitution.

### *Recent court challenges*

Two more recent court cases brought new life to the issues raised by the *Pocket Veto* and *Wright* cases. The first involved a challenge by Senator Edward Kennedy to a pocket veto exercised by President Nixon during a six-day Christmas recess in 1970 (the ten-day period for the bill, the Family Practice of Medicine Act, expired during the break). The bill had passed overwhelmingly in both chambers, and Nixon was immediately criticized for using the pocket veto inappropriately as a way to avoid an override vote. In a speech on the floor of the Senate, Kennedy argued that a pocket veto was not warranted because there had been no adjournment, and because Nixon had not been prevented from returning the bill (Condo, 1973: 395–96). Moreover, the pocket veto has been infrequently applied between congressional sessions (especially in recent years) and during recesses. Up until 1970, pocket vetoes during Christmas recesses had been applied only three times, all in the nineteenth century. Of the 187 pocket vetoes during the Truman, Eisenhower, and Kennedy administrations, 13 were applied during recesses. Also, the practice of calling an adjournment during a session of Congress rarely occurred before 1943. The absence of court challenges to other pocket vetoes in recent years is probably attributable to the fact that the bills involved were minor and/or uncontroversial ("The Veto Power and Kennedy v. Sampson," 1974: 602).

On August 9, 1972, Kennedy filed suit to compel publication of S.3418 as a law (*Kennedy v. Sampson,* 364 F. Supp. 1075 [D.D.C.1973]).[4] A federal district court ruled that Nixon had not been prevented from returning the vetoed bill to Congress, especially since the veto occurred in the middle of a congressional session. On appeal, the U.S. Court of Appeals expanded this ruling, raising doubts about pocket vetoes applied during any intrasession adjournment, as long as arrangements were made for receipt of possible veto messages (*Kennedy v. Sampson,* 511 F 2d 430 [D.C. Cir. 1974]). In refuting the *Pocket Veto* case, the appeals court also noted that congressional practices had changed dramatically since the 1920s. Lengthy adjournments were the norm up until that time. In fact, until 1818, Congress terminated all business not completed by the end of its first session. After 1818, the House allowed six days of the next session for completion of previous business. The Senate implemented this change in 1848. Shortly after that time, both houses dropped the six-day rule (Rogers, 1920: 21). By the 1970s, Congress was typically in session for nearly the entire year. Moreover, the state of communications is such that the logistical problems of past eras no longer exist ("The Veto Power and Kennedy v. Sampson," 1974: 607–11).

In a move that engendered significant public criticism, the solicitor general for the Nixon administration, Robert Bork, declined to appeal the case to the Supreme Court (Keeffe and Jorgenson, 1975: 755). The *Kennedy* case was significant because it was the first instance of a pocket veto being held unconstitutional and also because it pointed the way to the principle that the pocket veto could only be applied after *sine die* adjournments at the end of a Congress.[5]

During the 1970s, both the Ford and Carter presidencies abided by the principle of avoiding pocket vetoes during intra- and intersession adjournments, and Congress formalized procedures for receiving presidential messages during adjournments (Fisher, 1985: 152–53). This pattern changed during the Reagan administration. In December, 1981, Reagan pocket vetoed a relief bill for a Florida company between the first and second sessions of the Ninety-seventh Congress. The affected company contested the veto in court, but nothing came of the action.

A significant court challenge emerged from Reagan's pocket veto of a bill (HR 4042) designed to reinstate the requirement that the president certify to Congress every six months that El Salvador was making progress on human rights in order for it to continue receiving

American aid. The pocket veto occurred at the end of the first session of the Ninety-eighth Congress, in November, 1983. The veto prompted an immediate challenge by Congressman Michael D. Barnes and thirty-two other Democratic members of the House (the leaders of both parties in both houses later joined Barnes in the suit). On March 9, 1984, a U.S. District Court judge ruled in favor of the veto, citing the *Pocket Veto* case as the key precedent (rejecting the precedents in *Wright* and *Kennedy*) and saying that the pocket veto could be used between sessions of Congress (*Barnes v. Carmen,* 582 F. Supp. 163 [1984]).

This ruling was overturned on appeal by a court of appeals three-judge panel (*Barnes v. Kline,* 759 F.2d 21 [1985]). In a 2–1 decision, the majority ruled that the president may use the pocket veto only at the end of a two-year term of Congress. The pocket veto, said the court, "necessarily applies to the final adjournment by a Congress." The court was persuaded that, as long as Congress made arrangements to receive veto messages during adjournments and recesses, the practical problems of delay and uncertainty surrounding bill return cited in the *Pocket Veto* case could be easily remedied. Should the Congress decline to continue designating agents for receipt of messages (and it would certainly not be in Congress's interest to do so), the court said that the old *Pocket Veto* rule would again apply. In a sixty-three-page dissent, Judge Robert Bork (who, ironically, had defended this expanisve use of the pocket veto while serving as Nixon's solicitor general) argued that the courts should stay out of disputes between the other branches of government unless intervention was necessary to resolve suits resulting from the suffering of tanglible injuries. Bork declared that neither individual congressmen nor Congress as a whole could challenge the president's use of the pocket veto power.

The decision was appealed to the Supreme Court (*Burke v. Barnes,* 93 L Ed 2d 732). On January 14, 1987, the court ruled by a 6–2 vote (Justice Scalia took no part) that the case arising from the pocket veto of HR 4042 was moot, since there was no longer "a live case or controversy" (733). Writing for the majority (Justices Brennan, Marshall, Blackmun, Powell, and O'Connor), Chief Justice Rehnquist[6] concluded that "any issues concerning whether HR 4042 became a law were mooted when that bill expired by its own terms" (736). The date of expiration referred to was September 30, 1984. In the dissenting opinion Justice Stevens, joined by Justice White, argued strongly that the case was by no means moot. For the majority to assert that the issue was moot because the law had expired begs the very question of whether, in fact, the bill was a law in the first place, according to the dissenters. Congress had a valid interest in knowing whether HR 4042 was or was not a valid law both before and after the termination date of the legislation. If the bill was a valid law, Congress would have a clear interest in recovering funds allocated unlawfully to El Salvador, as well as in seeking compliance with other sections of the law.

In declaring the case moot, the majority vacated the judgment of the court of appeals, directing that court to remand the case to the district court with instructions to dismiss the complaint. In other words, the judgments of the two lower courts were, in effect, wiped from the books.

## Must presidents explain pocket vetoes?

The Constitution is clear in saying that, when the president returns a bill to Congress, he must do so "with his Objections," and the objections shall be entered "at large on their Journal." But since pocket vetoes are not returned, does it follow that no message or presidential explanation is necessary? In a nominal sense, messages are probably not required; they are, however, in keeping with the spirit of the Constitution, and are probably politically prudent, since an explanation for a pocket veto may help to soothe wounded political sensibilities.

In practice, presidents from Madison through Andrew Johnson issued explanatory messages for pocket vetoes in virtually all cases. The practice ceased with Grant, probably because of the increase in number (Grant pocket vetoed over one-and-a-half times as many bills as all of his predecessors combined), and because most of the affected bills involved private pension and related claims. The practice of issuing no public message (the 'silent pocket') persisted until 1934, when Franklin Roosevelt issued a formal statement declaring that henceforth, written messages would accompany pocket vetoes. According to Vose (1964: 397–400), the modern "memorandum pocket veto" arose as a consequence of the institutionalization of the presidency; that is, the presidency began, in the 1930s, to devote systematic attention to all aspects of the legislative process (as seen, most notably, in the rise of central clearance). This attention naturally included more careful attention to pocket vetoes. The practice of issuing memos of explanation has persisted to the present. By Vose's count, out of 447 pocket vetoes issued from 1934 to 1963, only four lacked accompanying messages. Since 1963, virtually all pocket vetoes have been accompanied by messages.

## When does the ten-day period begin?

The Constitution is rigid in allowing the president ten days (Sundays excepted) to consider legislation, regardless of whether he is in a position to apply a regular or pocket veto. Yet here, too, some confusion has persisted regarding the question of when the ten-day period begins. While some might suppose that the period begins when the second house passes the bill, it cannot be transmitted until the presiding officers of each chamber sign the bill (the time between passage and chamber leaders' signatures may be several days). The ten-day clock does not begin to tick, however, until the bill arrives at the White House and is "presented," in compliance with the presentment clause, to the president. Bills are, in actuality, presented to the Office of the Executive Clerk. Next to the office of the presidency itself, the Executive Clerk's Office is the oldest in the White House. On receipt of the parchment copy of the bill, it is stamped with the date of receipt. This day does not, however, count as the first day. The founding fathers were, in fact, clear on the understanding that the ten-day period would not begin until the day after receipt.[7]

This process raises a question concerning procedure when the president is out of the country or otherwise away from his duties for a significant period of time. During the early days of the Republic, this problem did not arise, as the president would be present in Washington throughout the congressional session. The issue arose in the twentieth century during Woodrow Wilson's term, as he was the first president to leave the hemisphere while in office. Wilson made an agreement with the speaker of the House and the president of the Senate that they would withhold their signatures from bills passed by Congress until Wilson returned to the U.S., allowing him to exercise the veto if he chose. Franklin Roosevelt made similar arrangements. In one instance, he signed a bill twenty-three days after Congress had adjourned (Corwin, 1957: 473, n.45, 46; 281).

When the president is away from Washington but still in the country, the ten-day period begins at the time of presentment to the White House. But what about when the president is abroad? This question resulted in a court case during the Eisenhower administration. On August 31, 1959, a bill was officially presented after Eisenhower had left for a trip to Europe. He returned on September 7 and vetoed the bill in question on September 14, more than ten days after the presentment date. Before leaving, however, Eisenhower had requested that presentment be delayed until his return. The veto was challenged in the court of claims (*Eber Bros. Wine and Liquor Corp. v. U.S. [337 F.2d 624 (Ct. Cl. 1964), cert. denied, 380 U.S. 950 (1965)]). The Court upheld the veto, ruling that during a presidential absence, the president could request (1) that Congress present bills to him personally abroad, (2) that Congress delay presentment until his return, or (3) that Congress present bills at the White House as if the president were there. Here again, the Eber* case conforms with the principle that every effort should be made to avoid circumventing the constitutionally prescribed final review of legislation by both president and Congress.

The issue of presentment and the ten-day period does not bear solely on the exercise of the pocket veto. It does show, however, how accommodation between the branches can resolve ambiguities and also how the courts can facilitate this process.

## Conclusion

The pocket veto represents an anomaly, as it is a kind of power the founders flatly rejected. Its presence in the Constitution is explainable only as presidential defense against abrupt, untimely congressional adjournment aimed at thwarting the president's ability to exercise the regular veto power. Of the several problems cited earlier in the chapter, most have been resolved through statute, tradition, and/or the courts.

One very important issue remains undecided, however. In 1987, the Supreme Court had the opportunity to clarify the circumstances under which the pocket veto can be used. In sidestepping the question by declaring the case moot, they also sidestepped reconciling past case precedent (from *Pocket Veto* to *Kennedy*) and changing congressional practices. Even the *Pocket Veto* case, cited as the principal support for freer use of the pocket veto, provides fuel for the conclusion that the pocket veto should be applied only at the end of a two-year Congress (Dumbrell and Lees, 1980). It emphasized the importance of granting the president adequate time to consider legislation; it pointed out (as did other cases) that the definition of adjournment was not important; that, instead, the question of whether the president was prevented from returning a bill *was* important; and that bills could not be left in limbo, because Congress, too, had a right and an obligation to deal with presidential objections in a timely, expeditious manner. Under modern circumstances of essentially year-round congressional sessions and improved methods of transportation and communication, these concerns are allayed. The one remaining stumbling block in the *Pocket Veto* case—that agents of Congress could not receive bills when the body was not in session—was flatly overruled in *Wright.* Moreover, even if a modern court returned to this principle, it would pose a glaring contradiction, as the presidency relies on agents to receive legislation from Congress and to perform other functions. The use of agents by Congress was proved reasonable and efficient in particular during the Ford and Carter administrations. President Reagan's more expansive application of the pocket veto simply illustrates a desire (not a need) to use an absolute veto instead of a return veto, and bears no relation to the purposes or necessities of the pocket veto power.

To argue that the pocket veto power should be applicable only at the end of a Congress is not to suggest the possibility of pushing the power out of existence altogether. Clearly, "the framers did not intend a presidential veto of legislation passed by one Congress to be considered, and possibly overridden, by another" ("The Veto Power and Kennedy v. Sampson," 1974: 594). Each two-year Congress is a distinct entity, even if the personnel remain largely the same from one to the next.

This chapter began by pointing out the differences between the regular and pocket vetoes. These differences might be restated by saying that the regular veto power can be imposed without restriction or qualification. The pocket veto, however, is highly circumstantial.

Its very existence is explainable only in the context of the circumstances that gave it rise and circumscribe its application. Given the changes in circumstances related to the pocket veto (longer sessions, legally designated agents, etc.), clarification and restriction of the power, whether by the courts, the legislature, or informal concurrence between president and Congress, can only be considered a reasonable adaptation that conserves the balance the framers sought.[8]

# 5

# The Item Veto Controversy

*The President is denied proper control over the federal budget. To remedy this, we support enhanced authority to prevent wasteful spending, including a line-item veto.*

Republican party platform, 1984

*The item veto is not (as often depicted) a simple, politically neutral device for bringing about economy and efficiency in government. It is first and foremost a political instrument and should be understood in this context.*

Ronald C. Moe (1985)

*Things are seldom what they seem, skim milk masquerades as cream.*

W. S. Gilbert
*HMS Pinafore*

In his State of the Union Addresses from 1984 to 1988, President Reagan requested that Congress grant him a power long sought by presidents. Resurrection of the idea that the president could and should have an item veto has stirred anew a controversy that itself reveals much about conceptions of the presidency. The vigor of this debate is seen in the sheer volume of public discourse since 1984 alone (examples of arguments for the item veto: Best, 1984, 1986; Palffy, 1984; *Wall Street Journal,* May 16, 18, 1984, October 21, 1986; Lambro, 1985; Mobil Oil ad in *New York Times,* March 7, 1985; Reynolds, 1985; examples of arguments against the item veto: Cronin,

1984; Paul, 1984; Zycher, 1984; *New York Times,* September 18, 1984, July 17, September 11, 1985; Broder, 1985; Cronin and Weill, 1985; Fisher, 1985, 1987; Leno, 1985; O'glove and Sobel, 1985; Ornstein, 1985; Spitzer, 1985, 1985a).

The item veto controversy spans both ideology and partisanship. Liberals and conservatives, Republicans and Democrats are to be found on both sides of this issue. Public opinion results yield decisive support for an item veto (in 1985, seventy-one percent favored the idea, according to a Gallup poll). Yet, members of Congress seem to agree that "it is hardly a burning issue and that few constituents understand what it would do" (Cohen, 1984: 274).

Most efforts to enact an item veto have attempted to do so by constitutional amendment. In 1985, however, Republican Senator Mack Mattingly proposed a bill granting the power by statute (S.43) and also by constitutional amendment (S.J. Res. 11; see appendix for copies of both).[1] The former route was proposed as a quicker and easier means than amendment to affect change, but doubt has been cast on the constitutionality of adopting any such change through regular legislation (Pear, 1984; Committee on Rules and Administration, 1985: 13–20; Zinn, 1951: 34).

## Definition

The term *item veto* (often erroneously called *line-item veto*—federal appropriations bills are not itemized line by line) refers simply to the power of an executive "to veto, delete or send back" (Cronin and Weill, 1985: 127) to the legislature some section or part of a bill, usually an appropriations bill. Item vetoes could apply, depending on how the power is defined, to appropriations bills (the norm for federal proposals) and/or other bills as well. An item veto could simply strike out a portion of a bill (disapproval) or it can be defined to reduce an appropriation. An amendatory veto, possessed by some governors, amounts to a conditional approval of a bill, pending adoption by the legislature of changes suggested by the governor. Though these variants exist in some states, our concern is with proposals to grant the president an item veto, which have generally taken the form of approval/disapproval of items in appropriations bills.

## Background

Our point of origin for examining the item veto is, as with other questions pertaining to the veto, the Founding Fathers. There is little doubt that the Constitution provides no authority for the president to exercise a selective veto (one allowing him to veto parts of a bill).[2] No debate on an item veto appears in the transcripts of the federal convention, and no formal proposal on the subject was offered. Yet, a significant debate on whether the founders would or would not have approved of an item veto has occurred in recent years. An elaboration of that debate, aside from its intellectual interest, will help to delineate the constitutional consequences of the contemporary debate over whether the president should be granted such power.

## Would the founders have approved?

The case that the Founding Fathers would have approved of an item veto is made strongly by my colleague Judith A. Best (1984; 1986). She argues that "the legislature has encroached on the veto power" and "has turned the tables on the executive making the veto work for legislative license instead of against it" (1984: 188). This state of affairs exists today, she says, primarily because of a legislative practice the founders did not envision: the attachment of riders and nongermane amendments to legislation. Existing veto powers do not allow presidents to weed out these additions, Best asserts, so presidents are sometimes faced with the unhappy choice of either vetoing an entire bill, thus "throw[ing] out the baby in order to get rid of the bath water," or signing the bill and acceding to expensive pork barrel projects or other riders that are "often either unsound or highly controversial" (187). The current veto power, she argues, is thus "warped and weakened" (183) since these legislative practices have converted "the qualified veto into something closely akin to the absolute veto, a device too rigorous to be used as a security against bad laws" (187). This weakening of the veto power means that our balanced constitutional system has been upset, since an important element in the "organic whole," the veto, has been diluted. Given its all-or-nothing quality, the existing veto is one that presidents are more reluctant to use. In this way, says Best, "the legislature has encroached on the veto power," rendering it less than useful. Therefore, it is "reasonable to assert that the Founders would not find the item veto to be a dangerous innovation but rather a rehabilitation of an original and essential check and balance" (188).

### *The rider problem*

The single most important factor spurring the call for item veto power has been the persistent practice by Congress of attaching riders and other nongermane amendments to legislation as a means to impel enactment and avoid a veto. It appears that this problem was not foreseen by the constitutional architects of the eighteenth century. One might suppose that the practice of 'tacking' (as the British called it) was or could have been known to the founders since it had been employed in the British Parliament, amidst much debate and acrimony, in the early 1700s (see chapter 1). Versed as they were in British law and history, the founders might well have been aware of the practice and either considered the problem unimportant, or the remedy superfluous. Still, lacking firm evidence, one cannot proceed on the assumption that the founders did, in fact, possess this insight.

Yet the rider problem emerged almost immediately under the new constitutional system. President Washington not only faced the problem but observed that the Constitution did not support anything resembling an item veto. "From the nature of the Constitution, I must approve all parts of a Bill, or reject it in toto" (Thomson, 1978: 31).

### *The revisionary nature of the veto*

Best makes much of the claim that, because of riders and the like, the modern veto is weakened because the president must either accept all or reject all of a bill presented to him. This Hobson's choice allegedly deters presidents from using the veto; thus, the item veto is necessary to restore the veto power to a more active posture. An obvious observation, however, is that, despite increasing legislative complexity (including attachment of riders), veto use has increased. In an aggregate, empirical sense, riders and other traits of modern legislation have not deterred veto use (see chapter 2). In fact, riders have encouraged veto use. More to the present point, however, the founders' conception of the veto power was one suited precisely to deal with the problem of riders. Though the veto is, in form, a

Hobson's choice, this assertion misstates what the founders had in mind. As discussed in chapter 1, the veto power was not viewed as simply a negative power to block or prevent. Referred to repeatedly as the "revisionary" power, it was seen as a tool for reconsideration and/or revision of legislation. This intent is seen also in the override provision, and in the requirement that the president provide written objections to explain vetoes. The veto was seen as an important tool for presidents to use to shape legislation. Such shaping could easily be the excision of riders objectionable to the president. Whether the veto has actually operated in this way in the last two hundred years or not, there is no question that this is the way the founders conceived of the veto power. As to the question of whether presidents have actually succeeded in using the existing veto against rider-laden legislation, chapters 2 and 3 summarize many such cases.

### *Checks and balances*

The founders constructed a system of limited government and shared powers. They were concerned with governmental paralysis (which they had experienced under the Articles of Confederation) but also with governmental aggrandizement. The historical record is relatively clear in showing that, in terms of possible abuses of power, the founders principally feared legislative excesses and abuses (Fisher, 1972: 21–22, appendix; Thach, 1969: 171). As Governeur Morris observed, the "Legislature will continually seek to aggrandize & perpetuate themselves; and will seize those critical moments produced by war, invasion or convulsion for that purpose" (Farrand, 1966: II, 52; I, 107).[3] This prediction highlights the historic irony that presidents, not the legislature, have succeeded in seizing critical moments to enhance their power. It is difficult, at best, to believe that the founders would have been sanguine about this presidential accumulation of powers, for we know that they also shared concern about executive excesses to the extent that a single executive was feared by some as a possible "foetus of monarchy" (Farrand, 1966: I, 66, 106–8). One cannot help but speculate that today's 'imperial presidency,' even (or especially) as resurrected after Watergate, would be a bit too monarchical for the tastes of the founders. The fact that the founders did not propose an item veto was cited by one analyst (Wilkinson, 1936: 109) as evidence not of their lack of awareness of the power, but rather as a symptom of their distrust of executive authority, recognizing that an item veto would give the president more leverage than do his existing veto powers.

Summarizing speculation on how an item veto would jibe with framers' intent, two considerations—the revisionary nature of the veto, and the vast accumulation of presidential powers, especially in this century—promote a conclusion that little justification of an item veto is to be found in framers' intent or constitutional construction. The item veto may, of course, be justified on other grounds. Those other arguments will be explored here as well. For the moment, our attention will turn to the origins and development of the item veto idea.

## Evolution of the clamor for the item veto

Presidential dissatisfaction with the bluntness of the all-or-nothing veto surfaced with the first president. But serious debate in Congress and elsewhere over legislation incorporating diverse components emerged first in the 1840s. These disputes may have contributed to the first appearance of a codified item veto power in the Confederate Constitution in 1861. First incorporated in the provisional constitution of February 8, the pertinent section (article I, section 5) gave the Confederate president the power to "veto any appropriation or appropriations, and approve any other appropriation or appropriations, in the same bill" (Wilkinson, 1936: 109). A slightly altered version of this power was incorporated in the permanent constitution, adopted March 11 (article I, section 7). The justification for inclusion of the item veto, offered by the provision's sponsor, was "to arrest corrupt or illegitimate expenditures," including "the habitual practice of loading bills . . . with reprehensible, not to say venal dispositions of the public money" (Ross and Schwengel, 1982: 69). Although Confederate President Jefferson Davis applied regular veto powers thirty-eight times (Mason, 1890: 210–13), he never exercised the item veto (Wells, 1924: 783).[4]

After the Civil War, the item veto was adopted by Georgia in 1865 and Texas in 1866. Thereafter, the idea spread rapidly to most of the other states by about 1915.[5] Today, forty-three of the fifty state constitutions include some kind of gubernatorial item veto.[6]

At the federal level, Ulysses Grant became the first president to call for item veto power. In his fifth annual message, delivered on December 1, 1873, he asked Congress to "authorize the Executive to approve of so much of any measure passing the two Houses of Congress as his judgment may dictate, without approving the whole, the disapproved portion or portions to be subject to the same rules as now" (*Messages,* 1913: VI, 4196). The stated purpose of the proposal was to "protect the public against the many abuses and waste of public moneys which creep into appropriation bills and other important measures" (4197). Perhaps the most pertinent observation about Grant's proposal is the close resemblence it bears to comparable contemporary proposals.

Three years later, the first concrete item veto proposal was submitted in Congress by Representative James C. Faulkner of West Virginia.[7] After Grant, Presidents Hayes, Arthur, and Cleveland all advocated an item veto, as have many twentieth-century presidents. By 1936, over eighty such proposals had been made. Up to the present, over a hundred and fifty item veto proposals have been offered. Their frequency notwithstanding, only one of these proposals was ever reported favorably out of congressional committee, and that occurred in 1884. The Senate, however, took no action on the bill.

## *The sound and the fury*

One cannot help but wonder why so much clamor for the item veto has not yielded more in the way of results, especially given the prevalence of the power in the states and persistent presidential advocacy. The answer can be found in the simple observation that the objections raised today against the power were also raised in the past. Heading the list was a pervasive concern about granting the president a prerogative that would only enhance his already substantial powers.

Though complaints against the congressional practice of attaching riders were frequent and not limited to presidents (e.g. Gibson, 1879: 5; Lockwood, 1884: 91), awareness was keen that the item veto represented a significant power. Writing in 1890 (137–38), veto analyst Edward C. Mason offered an evaluation of the item veto that bears repeating.

> This measure if adopted would not only increase the power of the veto, but also would practically destroy the only power which Congress now has over the President, apart from impeachment. . . . [T]he only coercion which Congress can make use of against the President, except by impeachment, is by tacking measures distasteful to the President to general appropriation bills, hoping in this way to compel him to assent to measures which, if presented on their own merits, would surely be vetoed.

Writing at about the same time, Lord Bryce (1891: 207–11) considered with great care the powers of the Congress over the executive. Of the two principal powers he discussed, impeachment and the power of the purse, he found the former to be rarely of any use: "[O]ne does not use steam hammers to crack nuts." Of the power of the purse, he concluded that Congress's ability to use this over the president was limited and less effective than it was for legislatures in European countries. Bryce cited the attempts of Congress to attach riders to legislation as its effort to influence the president. He observed the tactic to be successful against President Johnson but unsuccessful against President Hayes. Yet despite his observation that the congressional arsenal against the president was limited both in quantity of effective tools and in effectiveness, he also commented favorably on the item veto proposal, saying that it would "enable the executive to do its duty by the country in defeating many petty jobs," and would also diminish "wasteful expenditure on local purposes." Clearly, much of the appeal of the item veto, then as now, lay with its presumed efficacy in trimming budgetary fat.

On the other hand, Henry Jones Ford (1967: 185–86) noted in 1898 that the existing veto power, "in robust operation," could and had been used to item veto effect: "[U]nless it can be successfully contended that the items of appropriation bills obtain place and enactment without the vote of the two houses, they are fit subjects for the exercise of the veto power." Ford went on to cite an example of a different kind of action involving a presidential message issued by Grant, which had a similar, item veto effect. The president signed a river and harbor bill in 1876, but in an accompanying message to the House of Representatives, Grant declared that if he felt obliged to spend all of the money called for by the bill, he would have vetoed it. He made clear his intention to not spend money for any projects that were "of purely private or local interest" (*Messages,* 1913: VI, 4331). Such a de facto impoundment would be immediately challenged today. The example is noteworthy, however, because it is one of the two cited by Ford of presidents in the nineteenth century taking actions that had an item veto effect (the other being the regular veto).

Not all presidents have favored the item veto.[8] President Benjamin Harrison complained, as had other presidents, about the rider problem. Yet he accepted this lack of tidiness in legislating by noting that "many laws contain more than one proposition . . . and the President must deal with them as thus associated" (Harrison, 1897: 132). President Taft also commented on the problems posed for presidents by riders. Noting that an item veto "would be useful," he was "not entirely sure that it would be a safe provision. It would greatly enlarge the influence of the President, already large enough from patronage and party loyalty and other causes." Taft feared "a temptation to its sinister use by a President eager for continued political success." Even the impact on Congress of an item veto would be suspect, since it is "intended to pump patriotism into public officers by force" (Taft, 1967: 27–28).

More recently in this century, Franklin Roosevelt urged Congress to grant the item power because of the rider problem: "[T]his practice robs the Executive of legitimate and essential freedom of action in dealing with legislation" (Corwin, 1957: 475, n.55). Republican Senator Arthur Vandenberg (1936) shared these sentiments, though he looked forward to the time when such a power might be used to slash government spending. Since then, presidents Truman, Eisenhower, and Ford have also endorsed the idea (Cronin and Weill, 1985: 129).

The modern debate over the item veto, though enhanced in detail, has changed little in form from that of previous years. The pivotal arguments are summarized below.

## The item veto and the budget process

As the previous review of item veto advocacy illustrates, the drive to grant this power to the president has been and continues to be motivated substantially by the drive for greater frugality. Indeed, most item veto proposals are directed solely at appropriations measures.

The concern for the spiraling federal deficit, a perennial issue for the Republican party (e.g. Vandenberg, 1936), has taken on new urgency in the 1980s. In 1980, Ronald Reagan made a balanced budget a keystone of his campaign platform. He has also been a persistent advocate of a constitutional amendment calling for a balanced budget. In 1984, the issue was a theme, if not the key theme of the presidential campaign of Democrat Walter Mondale. The bipartisan adoption of this cause was accelerated in part by the fact that the total federal debt more than doubled during the Reagan presidency.

Leaving aside for the moment the problem of delineating items in appropriation or other bills so that they may in fact be subject to an item veto, advocates of the item veto point to the modern appropriations process as a monster out of control. In 1986, for example, Congress passed a record omnibus appropriations bill of $576 billion. Given appropriations of this scale, how can the president, or even Congress, claim to have control over the spending process? Columnist Donald Lambro (1985: 40–43) outlined a series of programs he found objectionable that were buried in some of the thirteen appropriation bills composing the almost $1 trillion 1986 budget. In Lambro's view, the president could weed out excessive programs to help bring spending under control with the stroke of an item veto pen.

Interestingly, the assessment of Lambro and others (see Subcommittee on the Constitution, 1984; Committee on Rules and Administration, 1985) that omnibus appropriations necessitate an item veto was also made by Republican Senator Arthur Vandenberg (1936: 11) over fifty years ago. "The modern congressional appropriation bill is a cross between a mammoth catchall, a grab bag, a jigsaw puzzle and an omelet." Vandenberg detailed several examples of what he called "Mother Hubbard Legislation"—bills filled with diverse, unrelated, and apparently extravagant spending programs. In point of fact, Congress has appropriated money through omnibus measures since the beginning of the country. As Louis Fisher (1987) notes, the first appropriation bill passed by Congress in 1789 was an omnibus bill, incorporating funds for both military and civilian programs. The same occurred in 1790 and 1791. Although the omnibus approach has not been the sole means of appropriation, it is as old as the country.

### *What could an item veto cut?*

Both proponents and critics admit that an item veto could only apply to a limited amount of spending. A House Budget Committee report (1984: 5–6) examined the projected 1985 budget, totalling $928 billion, and concluded that $503 billion of that amount would be exempt from an item veto, because of contractual, legal, or other obligations ($127 billion for interest on the national debt, $187 billion for social security, $92 billion for medicare and medicaid, and $97 billion for other mandatory programs). This would leave $263 billion in defense and $161 billion in discretionary nondefense spending. About $90 billion in defense and $78 billion in nondefense spending would be exempted from item veto because of prior commitments, leaving a total of $257 billion not protected (see also Committee on Rules and Administration, 1985: 57–59). Yet, given President Reagan's continued political commitment to defense spending above levels approved by Congress, he would not be expected to touch defense, leaving $90 billion vulnerable to item veto. In any given year, a president would be similarly prevented from vetoing either spending that is permanently authorized rather than appropriated or appropriations committed from previous years.

Defenders retort that Reagan might well carve out excess spending from defense if given a tool to do so. Moreover, the effects of the item veto are more properly examined cumulatively across several years, as legal and other existing obligations expire (Palffy, 1984). Still, an item veto would not bar the enactment of new contractual and legal obligations, though the regular veto could be used against such enabling legislation.

Ornstein (1985) argues, however, that an item veto might actually lead to increased spending levels. To illustrate, he cites the likely political consequences of item veto powers if President Reagan had had them in 1984 when Congress voted to trim twenty-five percent from the MX missile program. There is no reason to believe that Reagan, or any president in a similar circumstance, would refrain from threatening to item veto favored projects of wavering congressmen as a method of lining up votes. In this way, the end result could be an increase in government spending as the result of deals made to protect certain programs from the item veto.

## Porkys, two?

A leaner budget less heavily burdened with expensive, questionable pork barrel projects could be achieved with an item veto, advocates argue. Aside from helping the deficit problem, Congress's well-recognized habit of enacting programs of benefit to narrow constituencies (through mutual noninterference and logrolling) has been a longstanding point of contention between the executive and legislative branches. As chapter 2 detailed, such programs are partly responsible for the more prolific use of the veto by the president. Here, too, the connection between item veto advocacy and the desire to stem pork barreling is longstanding (e.g. "The President and 'The Pork Barrel,'" 1916: 178–80).[9] Presidents Arthur and Cleveland, for example, were vigorous in their denunciations of the congressional tendency to weigh down bills with pork riders. In fact, virtually all presidents have denounced this congressional tendency. Yet, given the remarkable historical persistence of pork barreling, we are led to two important questions: (1) Does the president have any interest in pork barreling; and (2) if the president had the item veto, can we accept at face value the assertion, so often repeated, that it would be used significantly to cut into such programs (leaving aside the obvious problem of defining what is and what is not wasteful, self-interested spending)?

There can be no doubt of the president's interest in pork barreling, distributive legislation, and in the patronage system in general (e.g. Riggs, 1973: 754). Like any elected official, the president has an obvious stake in electoral/popular support as well as support in Congress. Pork barrel projects can be extremely important in appealing to both of these constituencies. "While Congress can be viewed as a series of special-interest coalitions, the president is likely to respond, particularly in an era of weakened parties, to special interests in states that are large and competitive in the electoral college" (Zycher, 1984). Ornstein (1985: 110) points out that Reagan has supported such pork projects as subsidies for electric power and grazing lands in the West (his strongest political base), water projects that Carter fought to eliminate, the Clinch River breeder reactor, and farm subsidies and loan guarantees. Though some, or even all of these programs may be meritorious, they are indisputably classic examples of what is derisively labeled 'pork barrel.'

An empirical study of presidential policy-making in Congress covering the period 1954 through 1974 (Spitzer, 1983: 41–53, 98–100, 149–53) chronicles a major presidential commitment to distributive policy-making, noting in particular a marked rise in distributive policy proposals made by the president to Congress in every presidential election year during the time studied. Fisher (1985: 160) notes that the logrolling process, instrumental as a means of promoting patronage, is "no less characteristic of the executive branch" than of the legislative. There is no reason to believe that the president's interest in patronage policy is any smaller than that of Congress (e.g., Polsby and Wildavsky, 1980: 23). In fact, more often than not, "Congress has had to protect the public purse from Presidents pursuing expensive military objectives, wanting to buy more territory, or expanding federal involvement in commercial affairs" (Ornstein, 1985: 109). Speaking before a congressional committee, Ornstein was even more blunt in concluding that "any honest review of the historical record suggests that Congress has been more careful over the near 200-year history of this country with public money than Presidents have" (Committee on Rules and Administration, 1985: 193). This is not to suggest that pork is the principal concern of presidents, any more than it is for Congress; rather, it is to observe that presidential political and policy interests are not limited to high-minded, grandiose concerns induced from calculations of the truest national interest.

As to the second question of whether the president would in fact apply an item veto in a meaningful way to excise pork projects and other questionable concrete benefits, we can look to the past practices of presidents to conclude that it might well be applied in this fashion, at least under some circumstances. (This examination also raises an interesting question: If the existing veto has been applied in this fashion successfully, why does the president also need an item veto? This question will be addressed later.) However, other, less statesmanlike uses of the veto seem equally possible. Conservative Republican former Congressman Ron Paul (1984) noted about the item veto that "tremendous pressure could be put on Members of Congress who do not 'toe the line' with threats of appropriations of particular value to a Member's district [may be] deleted." Fisher (1985: 162) suggests how subtle coercion could be applied. "A presidential aide advises a member that the OMB is questioning a project in a bill before the President and then asks, as an aside, how the member plans to vote on the administration's bill for a vote next week." Similarly, presidents could reward supporters or wavering legislators by promising to shield a particular project from an item veto. Under these circumstances, the item veto could leave us with no less pork and maybe more. It would bias the legislative process more heavily in favor of the president's pork and that of his congressional allies. The only counterbalancing force would be the president's own self-restraint; but given the already-stated assertion of the president's interest in such measures, there is no reason to believe that more presidential authority in this area would lead to fewer partisan veto threats and/or less horse trading. The most plausible result would be a reduction of pork for the president's foes but an increase for his allies.

## The gubernatorial item veto as a model

One positive consequence of the item veto debate is that it has spurred research on state veto powers. Comparisons between state and federal practices are often useful in providing a clearer understanding of both. President Reagan employed the comparison when he requested an item veto in his 1987 State of the Union Address. "Give us the same tool that 43 governors have." Reagan has often referred to the power's usefulness to him while he served as governor of California.

The very prevalence of the power among the states, combined with the fact that no state has ever relinquished the power, seem to offer a prima facie case for its adoption at the federal level. Yet two questions warrant examination: (1) What has the state experience been? and (2) are there any important structural or other differences between federal and state executives that mitigate the comparison?

### *State experiences*

Testimonials of support from state leaders for the item veto are numerous (e.g., Wilkinson, 1936: 199–20). It has been endorsed by the National Conference of Mayors and the National Governors Association. Yet such testimonials reveal little of substance about the consequences of the item veto power in the states.

The first systematic examination of the state item veto (Wells, 1924) noted that the original purpose of the item veto provisions was to block appropriations considered improper or unconstitutional, as opposed to simply trimming excess expenditures. This concern was motivated in large part by the prevalent (and generally deserved) reputation of state legislatures as being both inept (passing hasty, ill-conceived legislation) and corrupt (subject to bribery, greed, and freebooting entrepreneurial activities) (Moe, 1985: 10–11). Legislative corruption receded in the twentieth century, but legislative irresponsibility did not. Wells (1924: 786) observed that the item veto "encouraged extravagance on the part of the law-making branch so that it came to rely upon the governor to make ends meet." Legislatures would often rush to finish their business at the end of a session, leaving the governor with the job of cleaning up. Yet the item veto was "insufficient to cope with the mounting costs of state government." At the same time, it could be used by governors "to reward or punish members of the legislature." Wells did not reject the item veto out of hand, but did conclude that it offered no budgetary panacea.

More recent analyses support the conclusion that the item veto is significant more for its political than budgetary consequences. A survey of legislative budget officers in the fifty states (Abney and Lauth, 1985) concluded that the item veto was generally a partisan instrument. Though it often resulted in budgetary reductions, this did not necessarily mean greater budgetary efficiency. They found it "easier to portray the item veto as an instrument of the executive increasing his or her legislative powers rather than as an instrument for efficiency" (377). A more limited study of the item veto in Wisconsin over a twelve-year period concluded similarly that the power "has been used primarily as a tool of policy choice and partisan advantage rather than of fiscal restraint" (Gosling, 1986: 292).

If the item veto is, as a spokesperson for the National Association of State Budget Officers observed, "more . . . a political tool to set different spending priorities" (Reinhold, 1985), what can be said of its actual budgetary consequences? An aggregate comparison of per capita spending (both statewide and combined state-local) noted that the seven states lacking item veto powers actually had lower levels of per capita expenditures than those states where the governors possess the power (Zycher, 1984). Cronin and Weill (1985: 146) compared non–item veto states with those having strong item vetoes. The group of seven states with a strong item veto had twice the per capita expenditure of those without. Although this comparison does not prove that an item veto causes higher spending, it certainly questions the efficacy of the item veto as an aid in reducing spending levels. The case of Governor Ronald Reagan is instructive in this regard.

As president, Reagan spoke often of the usefulness of an item veto as a means for slashing spending during his eight years as governor of California. Yet an analysis of his record as governor (O'glove and Sobel, 1985) yielded a dichotomy, repeated during his presidency, between rhetoric and action. As governor, Reagan presided over both the largest tax increase in California's history and an overall doubling of per capita taxes, while at the same time trumpeting the cause of frugality. In terms of his veto power (item and regular), he blocked a total of about $1.1 billion in spending as governor. Yet in his first two years in office as California governor, George Deukmejian vetoed $2.4 billion in spending bills (1984 and 1985 budget years). During his first two years as governor, Reagan blocked $175 million (controlled for inflation) in spending with the veto, one-fourteenth the amount blocked by Deukmejian. The case of Reagan reinforces the previous assessments of the item veto: The power brings with it no special palliative for budgetary woes.

### *The federal system versus the state systems*

State governmental systems nominally replicate the federal system. At the same time, no one would dispute the existence of important differences between the respective levels of government. The similarities, differences, and complexities as they relate to the item veto were explored by Fisher (1985a; see also Fisher and Devins, 1986) in terms of constitutions, budget procedures, state court rulings and political consequences. State constitutions are nearly uniform in their antilegislature bias. Proportionately, governors possess considerably greater power and prerogative. This relationship is evident in specific state constitutional authorization and appropriation strictures, which even go so far as to stipulate bill format and style. The purposes of these specific guidelines are to both restrict the legislatures and protect the gubernatorial item veto.

Budget procedures are also markedly different. At the state level, budgets are, in a true sense, executive budgets. Many state constitutions actually prohibit legislatures from tampering with the executive budget.

At the federal level, however, the budget is a legislative budget. Even after budgetary reform, the president's annual budget proposal is a set of recommendations, which Congress may alter as it sees fit. In fact, the evolution of federal budgeting reveals a conscious effort to avoid duplicating the executive-centered state systems. Moreover, budgeting at the state level is (by constitution, law, and practice) extremely specific and itemized. On the national level, however, both executive agencies and Congress prefer the lump-sum approach to appropriations as a means of facilitating administrative discretion. In an extremely detailed and thorough examination of over one hundred state court decisions concerning item veto powers, Fisher (1985a: 9–17) concluded that, despite almost one hundred years of litigation, the courts have been unable to resolve fundamental dilemmas concerning the nature and scope of item veto powers. "Courts are not closer to agreeing on the scope of the item-veto power than they were at the turn of the century" (22). In terms of political consequences, Fisher suggests that the item veto encourages legislative irresponsibility. When legislators know that an item veto waits at the end of the legislative labyrinth, they can accumulate political credits by approving larger appropriations for popular causes. In this way, complication of the budget process is politically and fiscally escalated.

In short, state legislative-executive relations are very different from those at the federal level. State legislatures are typically part-time bodies, meeting for only a few months out of the year. For this reason alone, state governors need greater authority. One study draws a distinction between federal and state veto use in this way: "At the national level, vetoes based on constitutional grounds and policy differences are the norm. In the states, the veto is used, in addition, because bills duplicate one another, because acts of legislatures are vague and incapable of enforcement, or because technical flaws have occurred in drafting" (Keefe and Ogul, 1981: 367). Moreover, an examination of some cases of state item veto use is less than comforting. Former Wisconsin Governor Patrick Lucey eliminated the word *not* in "not less than 50 percent" in a tourism appropriations bill he item vetoed while in office, transforming a 50-percent floor into a 50-percent ceiling. Lucey also 'vetoed' the *2* from a $25 million highway bond bill, thus reducing the authorization by $20 million (Harris and Hain, 1983: 410). Admittedly, these examples represent item veto powers greater than those generally contemplated for the president.

Nevertheless, the examples also suggest that a power such as the item veto can have unanticipated consequences and unanticipated reach.

Moe (1985) reached similar conclusions about the item veto. He argued that, based on state experience, a presidential item veto would result in tipping the political balance scales in the president's favor, increasing formal confrontation between the branches, spawning procedures designed to circumvent or neutralize the power, and engendering substantial new litigation between the branches. Most people would question the desirability of these consequences.

## The potency of existing veto powers

The president's constitutional veto powers are significant, but they also have limitations. Without doubt, the all-or-nothing quality of the veto limits its application. Still, the veto's record illustrates its potency seen particularly in the rise in the number of vetoes applied, the frequency of vetoes sustained, and in the ability of presidents to use the veto and veto threat to alter the course and content of legislation.[10] Admittedly, the veto is not always successful for the president, but if the founders had wanted a veto that was one-hundred-percent effective, they would have given him an absolute veto. Over-frequent use of the veto can be a costly strategy for the president. But here again, the veto was neither designed nor conceived of as an everyday power (e.g., Farrand, 1913: 184).

## Other powers that mimic the item veto

The fact that President Reagan or his predecessors would favor an item veto comes as no surprise. What is surprising is the lack of recognition that presidents already have a kind of item veto power. Presidents throughout history have succeeded in circumventing parts of statutes by referring to them as unconstitutional or be treating them as congressional suggestions rather than mandates through selective enforcement or by impounding funds. In the nineteenth century, presidents Jackson, Tyler, Buchanan, Grant, and Cleveland, for example, all employed one or the other of these first two devices (Fisher, 1978: 90–91; 1981: 25; Edwards, 1980: 91). Presidents in the twentieth century have been no less inclined to rely on these procedures. In 1976, for example, President Ford declared portions of a defense appropriations bill and a veterans bill a "nullity" at the time he signed them. His rationale in both cases was that the disputed provisions involved what were, in his view, improper legislative encroachments on executive powers (Fisher, 1978: 93). In 1979, President Carter decided to treat a statutory requirement as a recommendation in response to a congressional mandate that the U.S. establish consular relations at a specified time and place (Fisher, 1981: 25). Zinn (1951: 23–25) describes a related, longstanding practice (since Jackson) of presidents issuing memoranda elaborating on their interpretations of legislation at the time of signing. Although such memoranda cannot be used as a partial veto, presidents can and do offer specific construction to legislative ambiguities: "[T]here seems to be no constitutional basis for objecting to [the president's] expounding his views with respect to the bill."

More recently, President Reagan went beyond this tradition by actually attempting to interpret the legislative intent of the bill he was signing. His administration then expected courts to consider Reagan's signing statements when interpreting statutes. Though little noticed in the public press, this practice was sharply criticized as being a violation of separation of powers (Garber and Wimmer, 1987).

Impoundment has been used by presidents at least since the time of Jefferson. Despite recent restrictions, imposed on impoundment powers by the Budget and Impoundment Control Act of 1974, requiring close supervision and approval by Congress of budgetary rescissions (refusals to spend money) and deferrals (delays in spending money), presidents can still impede, alter, and even block the flow of funds to objectionable programs (Edwards, 1980: 21). President Ford, for example, requested no fewer than 330 deferrals and 150 rescissions. In spite of the 1974 budget act restrictions, fifty-nine percent of all presidential rescission requests from 1975 through 1984 have been approved by Congress (Fisher, 1978: 182; Palffy, 1984: 2; Committee on Rules and Administration, 1985: 57–58). Moreover, there can be little doubt that presidents continue to exert the dominant role in most aspects of budgeting, from the setting of budgetary priorities to the implementation of spending decisions (Fisher, 1975, passim; LeLoup, 1980: ch. 6). Cronin and Weill (1985: 133) itemize the president's powers over the budgetary process as including the submission of a balanced budget to Congress,[11] use of the veto, use of deferral and rescission authority, use of political negotiation and persuasion at all stages of the budgetary process, and use of the president's 'bully pulpit' to take his case over the heads of Congress directly to the American people.

## What constitutes an item?

Probably the most overlooked problem of the item veto proposal is the seemingly simple matter of determining what constitutes an item. Again, the states offer little guidance, as they "differ widely on how they define the term" (Cronin and Weill, 1985: 144). Moe (1985) raised a variety of questions and problems surrounding the nature and definition of item. For example, the frequently offered proposal to grant an item veto for appropriations raises the question of whether the veto would be applicable to provisions in appropriation bills that did not appropriate. Would it extend to appropriations not found in appropriations measures? If advocates prefer an item-reduction veto, how would it be applied to lump-sum appropriations, where the precise disbursement of money is dictated by informal agreements rather than by law? Could (or should) the president be able to apply an item veto to bill provisions that affected spending only indirectly? Accepting the assumption of most that entitlement programs would be exempted from the item veto, might Congress not be tempted to rely more on the entitlement approach (and similar backdoor means) to save programs from an item veto? When a bill or legislative package is constructed in Congress, it is often composed of interrelated parts. What ripple effects might item vetoes engender for ostensibly unrelated programs, including programs favored by the president? Given the disruption caused by an item veto, what would be the consequences of the likely delays on an already laborious legislative process? These and other ambiguities are not, by any means, new to the item veto debate (e.g., Subcommittee No. 3, 1957: 57–61); yet answers are no closer today than they were then.

One might assume that at least some of these problems could be resolved by careful drafting of a bill or constitutional amendment. Yet the conclusion of many of the analysts previously cited, as well as continuing confusion in the states, indicates that there is no simple resolution for these problems.

## Conclusion: "Things are seldom what they seem . . ."

If the item veto power were incorporated into the Constitution by amendment, questions of its constitutionality would obviously be moot. Nevertheless, considerations of the power's possible consequences—political, legal, constitutional—are entirely appropriate.

The thrust of that consideration in this chapter casts considerable doubt on most of the benefits ascribed to the item veto by its proponents. There is little doubt that an item veto would enhance the president's political influence over Congress. Some might welcome this change. However, the potency of the existing veto, combined with related powers as they pertain to lawmaking and budgeting, provide a more than ample arsenal for any modern president. To include an item veto in with the president's other substantial powers and prerogatives is to move even further away from a meaningful balance of powers. At best, it represents executive usurpation of legislative power, as it allows presidents to, in effect, rewrite legislation (e.g. Riggs, 1973: 756).

Moreover, every indication points to the likelihood that the item veto would aid the president in his politicking with Congress but its fiscal effectiveness would be marginal at best (as seen partly in the politically maximal, fiscally minimal consequences of the item veto for state governors). Congress has taken a 'bum rap' in the persistent accusation leveled by presidents and others that it is spendthrift. Up until 1980, most of the nation's debt had accumulated because of war. Add to that presidential spending initiatives and one is left with the conclusion that Congress's principal sin has been that of going along with the president. The intuitive plausibility of the assertion that an item veto would help trim size and fat from the budget bears little resemblence to the reality of probable consequences. There is no reason to believe that the item veto will magically transform the president into a fiscally-fit Jack LaLanne of the budget.

This leads us finally to the critical deception of the item veto proposal: It poses a constitutional solution for a political problem. A constitutional change in powers is neither necessary nor likely to be effective as a means to reduce spending, minimize riders, or combat waste. What *is* necessary is political will, especially on the part of the president. One of the ironies of the revival in the 1980s of the item veto debate is that it surrounds a president whose cries of budgetary anguish are prompted by a yawning federal deficit that was declining until the start of his term.[12] Since 1980, the debt's upward spiral is readily attributable to President Reagan's sweeping tax cut program, successful advocacy of marked increases in defense spending, and continued commitment to entitlement programs that lock in spending increases. Of these three barriers to budget reduction, only the third predated the Reagan administration. By the account of a former administration official (Stockman, 1986), the latter was largely embraced by the president despite the resistance of some of his advisers.

A final observation merits mention. Proposed structural changes are often defeated not for lack of merit but rather for lack of sufficient energy to overcome the enormous engine known as status quo. This engine has certainly worked against the item veto proposal, too. But the criticisms and qualifications summarized in this chapter amount to much more than a lame defense of 'the devil we know.' The presumed benefits of an item veto are neither proven nor consistent with available evidence. And if the Founding Fathers had approved of the consequences of such power for the president, they would have given us a very different chief executive in the first place.

# 6
# Conclusion

*The veto power . . . is a sort of appeal to the people. The executive power, which without this security might have been secretly oppressed, adopts this means of pleading its cause and stating its motives.*
Alexis de Tocqueville
*Democracy in America* (1835)

This book began with the straightforward proposition that the evolution of the presidential veto power is symptomatic of the rise of the modern strong presidency. Despite being one of the few powers of the president clearly enumerated in the Constitution, the veto has, in many ways, been overlooked as a central and important presidential power. Considerations of presidential powers invariably include an obligatory nod to the veto, but little more.

## From monarch to plebiscitarian

The founders were careful to establish a government of limited powers. Even so, they fretted about the potential for the abuse of power. They feared a tyrannical national legislature, but also the elevation of an autocratic monarch. The antiautocratic sentiment not only persisted, but if anything, intensified in the nineteenth century. Though the presidency of the 1800s was constrained by interpretation and precedent far more than that of this century, questions about the limits of presidential power and authority were no less germane. As the account in chapter 2 reveals, much of this debate centered on the presidential veto. Those who sided with the Whiggish interpretation of presidential power were quick to point to the vigorous use of the veto as a symptom of the kingly urges allegedly latent in American presidents. In a sense, the presidential critics were correct in drawing the analogy between British kings and presidents since the veto was for both the core executive power that connected them with the legislative process. The kingly veto was, by the eighteenth century, the last vestige of monarchical control over lawmaking, and the presidential veto, conceived of initially as a mechanism of presidential defense, provided an opening for a progressively greater presidential hand in the legislative process. The victory of the advocates of greater presidential involvement in their struggle with the Whigs is seen neatly in the fact that the relatively rare use of the veto by presidents like Jackson and Tyler was vigorously challenged, whereas by the end of the century frequent veto use was accepted essentially without challenge (aside from relatively routine disputes over particular bills). Contrary to the usual accounts, both strong *and* weak presidents played a role in the advancing presidential involvement in the legislative process via the veto. From acceptance of the veto itself came the veto threat, then congressional anticipation of the threat, then greater across-the-board anticipation of the president's legislative preferences.

Although both so-called strong and weak presidents advanced the boundaries of the institution, the effects of veto use by and on presidents were by no means uniform. Those presidents who possessed the attributes and resources so often attributed to 'strong' or 'great' presidents—a solid electoral mandate, enduring popular support, a strong partisan base in Congress, adroit personal political skills, etc.—benefited in two respects: (1) The possession of these power resources meant that they were not compelled to rely on the veto as a primary or sole weapon in their dealings with Congress; and (2) they were most able to withstand the negative political fallout that accompanies the perception of frequent veto use. Those presidents who lacked some or all of these resources—because of accidental ascension to the presidency, intractable contemporary issues, the absence of personal leadership skills, etc.—were often compelled to fall back on a veto strategy that, even if successful in the short term, usually had detrimental consequences. Indeed, though unrestricted (in a constitutional sense) veto use came to be accepted, it was and is a power that entails built-in political costs regardless of who uses it. In the short term, the veto is a convenient and effective weapon. But used with frequency over time, its cumulative costs are substantial. Political opponents of the president readily understand that it represents an inability on the part of the president to block or alter legislation before it reaches his desk. Yet, despite the costs of a veto strategy for those presidents who employed it, the long-term effect was to extend the boundaries of the presidency. Such executives as Tyler, Andrew Johnson, Arthur, and Hayes advanced the cause of the modern strong presidency just as surely (though differently) as Jackson, Lincoln, Wilson, and the Roosevelts. Reliance on the veto by unassertive presidents in noncrisis circumstances may have politically hurt those particular presidents, but it increased the power of the presidency.

The rise of veto use was also accompanied by the advance of an ironic argument. Despite its monarchical, inherently antimajoritarian nature (how else can one view a power that allows a single individual to thwart the actions of a large, representative group?), the veto was increasingly and successfully defended as a weapon used on behalf of the people. Predicated on the president's national constituency, chief executives promoted particular vetoes as both the voice of the people and an appeal to the same. Although not all appeals were equally effective, their cumulative impact helped enforce the plebiscitarian quality of the presidential office and the veto power.

## The veto: power and symbol

The modern veto power possesses a dual quality. As a substantive power, it is potent, but politically dangerous for presidents who use it too much. The veto also has a symbolic quality that, though ethereal, can be highly useful to presidents. The distinction between these two qualities is exemplified in the Ford and Reagan presidencies. Because of circumstances largely beyond his control, President Ford was the first president in this century compelled to rely on a true veto strategy. Ford lacked his own electoral mandate and suffered from ties to Nixon, the ripple effects of Watergate, and a hostile Congress. His veto success rate was high, but so were the costs. The Reagan administration, on the other hand, had little need for frequent veto use. Still, the symbolic veto was present in the rhetoric of the Reagan presidency. It was evidenced in persistent claims of the need for an item veto; in expansive interpretation of the pocket veto; in frequent use of veto threats; and in the confrontational style that dared Congress to step across an imaginary line drawn in the Washington political dust. Though the political impact of such bluff and bluster is variable, its political costs have been minimal for Reagan. If nothing else, these rhetorical tactics advance the periphery of the presidential power debate.

Perhaps the most important lesson to be drawn from the Ford and Reagan cases is that the consequences of veto use for them bear such close resemblence to consequences for presidents in previous eras. As a power etched into the constitutional framework, the veto continues to reveal characteristics that span individual presidencies and particular eras. As the case of the veto power makes clear, the Constitution continues to set the baseline for the institutional and political patterns that govern America.

# APPENDIX

99TH CONGRESS
1ST SESSION

## S. J. RES. 11

Proposing an amendment to the Constitution of the United States to allow the President to veto items of appropriation.

---

IN THE SENATE OF THE UNITED STATES

JANUARY 3, 1985

Mr. MATTINGLY (for himself, Mr. EVANS, Mr. THURMOND, and Mr. ARMSTRONG) introduced the following joint resolution; which was read twice and referred to the Committee on the Judiciary

---

## JOINT RESOLUTION

Proposing an amendment to the Constitution of the United States to allow the President to veto items of appropriation.

1 *Resolved by the Senate and House of Representatives*
2 *of the United States of America in Congress assembled*
3 *(two-thirds of each House concurring therein),* That the fol-
4 lowing article is proposed as an amendment to the Constitu-
5 tion, which shall be valid to all intents and purposes as part

1 of the Constitution when ratified by the legislatures of three-
2 fourths of the several States within seven years after the date
3 of its submission to the States for ratification:
4
5 "ARTICLE—
6 "The President may disapprove any item of appropria-
7 tion in any Act or joint resolution. If an Act or joint resolu-
8 tion is approved by the President, any item of appropriation
9 contained therein which is not disapproved shall become law.
10 The President shall return with his objections any item of
11 appropriation disapproved to the House in which the Act or
12 joint resolution containing such item originated. The Con-
13 gress may, in the manner prescribed under Section 7 of Arti-
14 cle I for Acts disapproved by the President, reconsider any
15 item of appropriation disapproved under this Article.".

□

99TH CONGRESS
1ST SESSION

# S. 43

To provide that each item of any general or special appropriation bill and any bill or joint resolution making supplemental, deficiency, or continuing appropriations that is agreed to by both Houses of the Congress in the same form shall be enrolled as a separate bill or joint resolution for presentation to the President.

---

IN THE SENATE OF THE UNITED STATES

JANUARY 3, 1985

Mr. MATTINGLY (for himself, Mr. EVANS, Mr. BIDEN, Mr. THURMOND, Mr. ARMSTRONG, and Mr. KASTEN) introduced the following bill; which was read twice and referred to the Committee on Rules and Administration

---

# A BILL

To provide that each item of any general or special appropriation bill and any bill or joint resolution making supplemental, deficiency, or continuing appropriations that is agreed to by both Houses of the Congress in the same form shall be enrolled as a separate bill or joint resolution for presentation to the President.

1 *Be it enacted by the Senate and House of Representa-*
2 *tives of the United States of America in Congress assembled,*
3 That (a)(1) notwithstanding any other provision of law, when

1 any general or special appropriation bill or any bill or joint
2 resolution making supplemental, deficiency, or continuing ap-
3 propriations passes both Houses of the Congress in the same
4 form, the Secretary of the Senate (in the case of a bill or joint
5 resolution originating in the Senate) or the Clerk of the
6 House of Representatives (in the case of a bill or joint resolu-
7 tion originating in the House of Representatives) shall cause
8 the enrolling clerk of such House to enroll each item of such
9 bill or joint resolution as a separate bill or joint resolution, as
10 the case may be.
11 (2) A bill or joint resolution that is required to be en-
12 rolled pursuant to paragraph (1)—
13 (A) shall be enrolled without substantive revision,
14 (B) shall conform in style and form to the applica-
15 ble provisions of chapter 2 of title 1, United States
16 Code (as such provisions are in effect on the date of
17 the enactment of this Act), and
18 (C) shall bear the designation of the measure of
19 which it was an item prior to such enrollment, together
20 with such other designation as may be necessary to
21 distinguish such bill or joint resolution from other bills
22 or joint resolutions enrolled pursuant to paragraph (1)
23 with respect to the same measure.
24 (b) A bill or joint resolution enrolled pursuant to para-
25 graph (1) of subsection (a) with respect to an item shall be
26 deemed to be a bill under Clauses 2 and 3 of Section 7 of
27 Article 1 of the Constitution of the United States and shall be
28 signed by the presiding officers of both Houses of the Con-
29 gress and presented to the President for approval or disap-
30 proval (and otherwise treated for all purposes) in the manner
31 provided for bills and joint resolutions generally.
32 (c) For purposes of this concurrent resolution, the term
33 "item" means any numbered section and any unnumbered
34 paragraph of—

1 (1) any general or special appropriation bill, and
2 (2) any bill or joint resolution making supplemen-
3 tal, deficiency, or continuing appropriations.
4 (d) The provisions of this Act shall apply to bills and
5 joint resolutions agreed to by the Congress during the two-
6 calendar-year period beginning with the date of the enact-
7 ment of this Act.

□

# NOTES

## Chapter 1

1. Mason (1890: 16) speculates that this may have inspired the authors of the Massachusetts Constitution in inserting a 'suspensive veto'—i.e., one capable of being overridden—into the document, an idea which later became part of the federal Constitution.

2. For arguments that the veto is not dead (despite Walter Bagehot's oft-quoted axiom that if Parliament passed the Queen's death certificate, she would be obliged to sign it) and discussion of circumstances under which it might reemerge, see Hearn (1867): 62–63; Jennings (1959): 545; Chrimes (1965): 14.

3. The New York Council of Revision operated until 1821, when veto powers were consolidated in the hands of the governor alone. In that time, 169 bills had been vetoed out of 6,590 presented. Fifty-one vetoes were overridden (Benton, 1888: 61). For an exhaustive history of the gubernatorial veto in New York, see Prescott and Zimmerman (1980).

4. Vermont drew up a constitution in 1777 after driving the British out, but it did not become a state until 1791, when it became the fourteenth.

5. The term *veto* is sometimes applied in ways that seem to take it far from a more precise political meaning. For purposes of this study, the concept of *veto* applies to the ability of one actor to block or 'veto' the completed actions of another actor, as when the president blocks a bill approved by Congress, or the British king blocks an act of Parliament. The first extended definition of *veto* in the Oxford English Dictionary refers to *veto* as "the word by which the Roman tribunes of the people opposed measures of the Senate or actions of the magistrates." Even though many actors in the Roman Republic could veto, this definition clearly alludes to the blocking of the action of one actor or institution by another. Thus, to say that a member of Congress could veto a bill during the time of the Articles of Confederation is, by this definition, an overly broad use of the term.

6. One recent observer argues that the founding fathers "had inserted the veto to thwart rather than represent the 'popular will' " (Pessen, 1975: 135). Aside from the underlying elitist attitudes of many of the framers, there is no particular evidence to suggest that this was a motivation. If anything, a few in the convention thought that the president could represent the popular will through his veto in circumstances when the legislature failed to do so.

7. Balloting at the convention was conducted by state.

8. This may seem to some to be semantic nitpicking. But as the careful avoidance of the word *veto* illustrates, the founders were sensitive to such word use.

9. As Zinn (1951: 22) observed, the historic exercise of the veto "has not followed the course set for it in the Constitution but has worked out a path different in direction and extent from that prophesied." See also Mason (1890): 139, and update of Mason by Towle (1937).

## Chapter 2

1. Interestingly, neither Adams nor Jefferson participated in the 1787 convention. Whether this bore any relation to the absence of vetoes is a matter of pure speculation. One cannot claim, however, that they declined to use the veto because of their memories of the convention debates relating to the subject.

2. The Clay-Jackson feud extended back to the presidential election of 1824, when the election was thrown into the House of Representatives. Clay threw his support to John Quincy Adams instead of Jackson, giving Adams the election despite Jackson's higher popular vote total.

3. See *The Pocket Veto Case* (1929) (279 U.S. 655). The court ruled that congressional adjournment at the end of a session prevented the return of a bill.

4. The motion to censure read: "*Resolved,* That the President in the late executive proceeding in relation to the public revenue, has assumed upon himself authority and power not conferred by the Constitution and laws, but in derogation of both." (*Congressional Globe,* March 28, 1834: 271)

5. Kent first proposed this amendment on December 24, 1833 (*Debates*: 58). Clay spoke against this motion in 1833, on the grounds that the nation's poor economic situation was a higher priority. Clay strongly supported this proposal subsequently.

6. This was a well-founded criticism. The lyrics of a campaign song of the time included these words: "We'll go for Tippecanoe and Tyler

too, Without a why or wherefore." Whigs sought to suppress issues because of deep rifts within the party.

7. Neither of the two standard works on the veto (Mason, 1890; Jackson, 1967) mention this first successful override.

8. The Constitution says a veto shall be overridden if passed by "two-thirds of that House"; in the Constitution, the word *House* is synonymous with quorum (see Constitution, art. I, sect. 5).

9. There were those whose criticism of executive power was more harsh. The best example is a book by Henry C. Lockwood, a member of the New York Bar, entitled *The Abolition of the Presidency* (1884). Lockwood's treatise is an indictment of the presidency as a whole, which he views as too monarchical and imperial. His criticism of the veto power is but a part of this larger castigation. He proposes a return to the pre-1787 governance system of a dominant legislature and no single, independent executive.

10. This observation is not offered as a critique of Congress's representation function, nor as an undue elevation of the president's role.

11. The concept of the plebiscitary presidency is discussed in Lowi (1985), Ch. 5.

12. This policy category is one of four originally suggested by Lowi (1964). See also Spitzer (1983), Ch. 2.

## Chapter 3

1. From correspondence with Stephen J. Wayne. He also noted that "there is even some position-taking for the record to demonstrate consensus within the administration."

2. In a television panel discussion held in 1986 on public broadcasting titled "The Presidency and the Constitution: The Budget Crunch," former President Ford offered this perspective on the veto: "Now, I happen to believe that the veto's not a negative thing. It's in the Constitution. And a president ought to use it more freely if he doesn't like what the Congress is doing up there. What difference does it make if he gets overridden? He makes the point that the Congress is the body in our government that has taken this course of action. The only way you're going to get the budget under control is for a president to establish whatever priorities he believes in, fight for them, and veto, veto, veto."

3. Information drawn from *Congressional Quarterly Annual Almanac, Congressional Quarterly Weekly Reports, Presidential Vetoes, 1789–1976,* and newspaper accounts.

4. The figures presented here represent rough approximations, as it is difficult to assess with precision the exact spending that results from many bills, especially those calling for multiyear spending.

5. These date taken from Spitzer, 1985: 617, n. 29, and update by the author. I am indebted to Thornton O'glove for his support and encouragement in pursuing this line of investigation.

6. My thanks to Jim Cullen for his help in gathering preliminary information on these two cases.

7. Arms sales such as this were originally subject to congressional disapproval by legislative veto (a move to disapprove that did not cross the president's desk). The disapproval procedure was modified after the Supreme Court struck down the legislative veto in *Immigration and Naturalization Service v. Chadha* (1983).

8. From 1789 to 1984 (according to Copeland, 1983; update by author), 179 public bills were vetoed by presidents in their first year of their term (incorporating first and second terms), 293 in their second year, 249 in their third year, and 301 in the fourth (presidential terms are defined here as a four-year cycle, regardless of when the president entered the cycle). See also Hoff (1987).

9. My thanks to Pam Klein for her careful preliminary work on this data.

## Chapter 4

1. See "The Veto Power and Kennedy v. Sampson" (1974: 592). "Because in the Constitution '[e]very word appears to have been weighted with the utmost deliberation,' . . . it cannot be said that the pocket veto, as an absolute negative, was unintended by the framers." (n.19)

2. The docket title of the case is *The Okanogan, Methow, San Poelis, Nespelen, Colville, and Lake Indian Tribes or Bands of the State of Washington v. U.S.;* or, *Okanogan v. U.S.*

3. By a more recent count, twenty-five of the thirty presidents up to and including Nixon who have used the pocket veto have exercised it during intercession adjournments in 272 instances (*Barnes v. Kline,* 759 F.2d 21 [1985]: 39). In citing this data as seeming to support such use of the pocket veto, the appeals court also noted that this past practice did not resolve the queston of the use of pocket veto power by modern presidents, since intersession adjournments formerly averaged five to six months in duration, whereas they now average four weeks or less.

4. For more on the Kennedy challenge and a good background on the pocket veto controversy, see Subcommittee on the Separation of

Powers (1971). See also Bellamy (1972), Kass (1971), and the Presidential Veto Power (1971). Early treatment of pocket veto issues is found in Cohen (1930), and Serven (1929).

5. Kennedy also challenged Nixon's pocket veto of an urban mass transit bill, rendered between the first and second sessions of the Ninety-third Congress, on December 22, 1973 (*Kennedy v. Jones,* 412 F. Supp. 353 [D.D.C. 1976]). But on April 13, 1976, the Ford administration consented to the entry of judgment in favor of Kennedy. According to at least one constitutional law expert (Cooley, 1931: 148, n.36), "it seems quite clear that the word 'adjournment' . . . means the final adjournment of the Congress itself and not the adjournment of one of its sessions."

6. While serving as assistant attorney general under President Nixon, Rehnquist defended Nixon's expansive interpretation of the pocket veto power. See Subcommittee on Separation of Powers (1971: 5–10, 194–96).

7. I am indebted to Daniel J. Marks of the White House Office of Executive Clerk for this information.

8. In a report presented to the House Judiciary Committee in 1951 (Zinn: 39), a proposal to legislate a definition of adjournment read this way: " '[A]djournment' means an adjournment sine die by both the Senate and the House of Representatives terminating a session of the Congress." The words "session of the" could easily be dropped to indicate that adjournment for purposes of the pocket veto applied to the end of a two-year Congress. Fisher (1985: 152) also sees this as a logical resolution of the pocket veto dispute.

## Chapter 5

1. Efforts to promote the item veto were probably dampened by the fact that Mattingly, its prime proponent in the Senate, was defeated for reelection in 1986. For more on the item veto, see American Enterprise Institute (1984), Bach (1984), and Symposium on the Line-Item Veto (1985).

2. A law journal article (Givens, 1965) argues that if the president attempted to veto a rider that bore no relation to the bill to which it was attached, such a veto might be upheld by the courts. This novel argument is predicated on a definition of *bill* which refers to an interconnected piece of legislation dealing with the same or related subjects. This argument was challenged by Riggs (1973), who argues that such a selective veto would be an unconstitutional violation of separation of powers.

3. For more on the fears of legislative aggrandizement, see the comments of Wilson, Hamilton, and Madison at the federal convention.

4. *The Wall Street Journal* reported erroneously that President Davis "used the [item veto] power . . . effectively" ("Bring Back the Veto," October 21, 1986).

5. Changes in state veto powers up to 1917 are carefully noted in Fairlie (1917) and Moe (1985). See also Beckman (1957).

6. Those state constitutions that do not include an item veto for their governors are Indiana, Maine, Nebraska, New Hampshire, Rhode Island, and Vermont. North Carolina provides no veto whatever for its governor.

7. H.R. 46, forty-fourth Congress, First Session, introduced on January 18, 1876.

8. Among modern presidents, Carter has reversed his position on the item veto, and now has doubts about it (Cronin and Weill, 1985: 130).

9. The Prohibition party platform of 1916 was the first to call for an item veto to cut "pork barrel."

10. Advocates of the item veto have recognized the item veto effect of the existing veto. For example, Vandenberg (1936: 11) cited the case of President Wilson's three vetoes of omnibus appropriations bills (one of them three days before the end of the session), prompted by his desire to eliminate objectionable provisions. Though these vetoes could have brought government to a halt, Wilson succeeded in forcing the desired changes. Vandenberg cited the example to illustrate the difficulty and clumsiness of using the veto in this way.

11. Despite Reagan's strident criticism of Congress, year-by-year comparisons of Reagan's proposed budgets with those enacted reveal little difference between them (Committee on Rules and Administration, 1985: 53–56).

12. Measured as a percent of the gross national product.

# REFERENCES


Abney, Glenn, and Thomas P. Lauth. 1985. The Line-Item Veto in the States: An Instrument for Fiscal Restraint or an Instrument for Partisanship? *Public Administration Review* 45(May/June):372–77.

Adams, George Burton. 1934. *Constitutional History of England.* New York: Henry Holt & Co.

Administration's Role: How Much Is Enough? 1986. *Congressional Quarterly Weekly Report,* June 21.

American Enterprise Institute. 1984. *Proposals for Line-Item Veto Authority.* Washington, D.C.: American Enterprise Institute.

Annals of Congress. 1791–1824.

Bach, Stanley I. 1984. Interpreting and Implementing Item Veto Proposals. *Congressional Research Service, The Library of Congress,* February 4.

Beard, Charles A. 1914. Veto Power. *Cyclopedia of American Government,* vol. 3. New York: Appleton & Co.

Beckman, Ada E. 1957. The Item Veto Power of the Executive. *Temple Law Quarterly* 31(Fall):27–34.

Bellamy, Calvin. 1972. The Growing Potential of the Pocket Veto: Another Area of Increasing Presidential Power. *Illinois Bar Journal* 61(October):85–91.

Benton, Josiah H. 1888. *The Veto Power in the United States: What Is It?* Boston: Addison C. Getchell.

Berdahl, Clarence A. 1937. The President's Veto of Private Bills. *Political Science Quarterly* 52(December):505–31.

Best, Judith A. 1984. The Item Veto: Would the Founders Approve? *Presidential Studies Quarterly* 14(Spring):183–88.

_______. 1986. Restore President's Power Over the Purse. *Wall Street Journal,* October 21.

Binkley, Wilfred E. 1958. *The Man in the White House.* Baltimore, MD: Johns Hopkins Press.

_______. 1962. *President and Congress.* New York: Vintage Books.

Black, Charles L. 1976. Some Thoughts on the Veto. *Law and Contemporary Problems* 40(Spring):87–101.

Both Chambers Say 'No' to Saudi Arms Deal. 1986. *Congressional Quarterly Weekly Report,* May 10.

Broder, David. 1985. Budget Line-Item Veto a Bad Idea. *Utica Daily Press,* July 24.

Bryce, James. 1891. *The American Commonwealth,* 2 vols. New York: Macmillan.

Bucking Strong Hill Sentiment, Reagan Vetoes South Africa Bill. 1986. *Congressional Quarterly Weekly Report,* September 27.

Buckland, W. W. 1925. *A Manual of Roman Private Law.* Cambridge: Cambridge University Press.

Burns, James MacGregor. 1956. *Roosevelt: The Lion and the Fox.* New York: Harcourt, Brace and Jovanovich.

Burton, David R. 1984. If Congress Is Spendthrift, Where Are Reagan's Vetoes? *Wall Street Journal,* September 11.

Chitwood, Oliver. 1964. *John Tyler.* New York: Russell and Russell.

Chrimes, S.B. 1965. *English Constitutional History.* London: Oxford University Press.

Clineburg, William A. 1966. The Presidential Veto Power. *South Carolina Law Review* 18:732–754.

Cohen, Harold. 1930. Validity of Pocket-Veto. *Boston Univeristy Law Review* 10(January):76–81.

Cohen, Richard E. 1984. Congress Plays Election-Year Politics with Line-Item Veto Proposal. *National Journal,* February 11, 274–76.

Committee on the Budget. 1984. The Line-Item Veto: An Appraisal. U.S. House of Representatives, 98th Cong., 2d sess., February. Washington, D.C.: U.S. Government Printing Office.

Committee on Rules and Administration, Hearings. 1985. Line Item Veto. U.S. Senate, 99th Cong., 1st sess., May 14, 20, June 20. Washington, D.C.: U.S. Government Printing Office.

Condo, Joseph A. 1973. The Veto of S.3418: More Congressional Power in the President's Pocket? *Catholic University Law Review* 22:385–402.

Congress Shoots Down a Saudi Missile Sale. 1986. *U.S. News and World Report,* May 9.

Congressional Globe. 1834–1873.

Congressional Record. 1873–present.

Conkling, Frederick A. 1890. Abuses of the Veto Power. *The Forum* 8(January):555–65.

Cooley, Thomas M. 1931. *Constitutional Law.* Boston: Little, Brown.

Copeland, Gary. 1983. When Congress and the President Collide: Why Presidents Veto Legislation. *Journal of Politics* 45(August):696–710.

Corwin, Edward S. 1957. *The President: Office and Powers.* New York: New York University Press.

Cronin, Thomas E. 1984. The Item Veto: An Idea Whose Time Shouldn't Come. *Christian Science Monitor,* September 4.

Cronin, Thomas E., and Jeffrey J. Weill. 1985. An Item Veto for the President? *Congress and the Presidency* 12(Autumn): 127–51.

Curtis, George T. 1889. *Constitutional History of the United States,* 2 vols. New York: Harper and Bros.

Davidson, Roger H. 1984. The Presidency and Congress. *The Presidency and the Political System,* ed. Michael Nelson. Washington, D.C.: Congressional Quarterly Press.

Debates in Congress. 1824–1833.

Dicey, Albert V. 1927. *Introduction to the Study of the Law of the Constitution.* London: Macmillan.

Dumbrell, John W., and John D. Lees. 1980. Presidential Pocket-Veto Power: A Constitutional Anachronism? *Political Studies* 28(March):109–16.

Edwards III, George C. 1980. *Presidential Influence in Congress.* San Francisco: W.H. Freeman.

Encyclopaedia Britannica, 11th ed. 1910–1911. Veto. Vol.28:14–15.

Fairlie, John A. 1917. The Veto Power of the State Governor. *American Political Science Review* 11(August):473–93.

Farrand, Max. 1913. *The Framing of the Constitution.* New Haven: Yale University Press.

_______. 1966. *The Records of the Federal Convention of 1787,* 4 vols. New Haven: Yale Univeristy Press.

*Federalist Papers.* 1961. New York: New American Library.

Finer, Herman. 1960. *The Presidency.* Chicago: University of Chicago Press.

Fisher, Louis. 1978. *The Constitution Between Friends.* New York: St. Martin's Press.

_______. 1985. *Constitutional Conflicts Between Congress and the President.* Princeton, NJ: Princeton University Press, 1985.

_______. 1987. The Item Veto—a Misconception. *Washington Post,* February 23.

_______. 1985a. The Item Veto: The Risks of Emulating the States. A paper delivered at the 1985 Annual Meeting of the American Political Science Association, New Orleans, LA, August 29–September 1.

_______. 1981. *The Politics of Shared Power.* Washington, D.C.: Congressional Quarterly Press.

_______. 1972. *President and Congress.* New York: Free Press.

_______. 1975. *Presidential Spending Power.* Princeton, NJ: Princeton University Press.

Fisher, Louis, and Neal Devins. 1986. How Successfully Can the States' Item Veto Be Transferred to the President? *Georgetown Law Journal* 75(October):159–97.

Ford, Henry Jones. 1921. *The Cleveland Era.* New Haven, CT: Yale University Press.

Ford, Henry Jones. 1967. *The Rise and Growth of American Politics.* New York: DaCapo Press.

Garber, Marc N., and Kurt A. Wimmer. 1987. Presidential Signing Statements As Interpretations of Legislative Intent: An Executive Aggrandizement of Power. *Harvard Journal on Legislation* 24(Summer):363–96.

Gattuso, James, and Stephen Moore. 1985. Reagan's Trump Card: The Veto. *Heritage Foundation Backgrounder,* July 8.

Gibson, Randall L. 1879. *A Free Ballot the Only Safeguard of Free Institutions.* Washington, D.C.

Givens, Richard A. 1965. The Validity of a Separate Veto of Nongermane Riders to Legislation. *Temple Law Quarterly* 39(Fall):60–64.

Gosling, James J. 1986. Wisconsin Item-Veto Lessons. *Public Administration Review* 46(July/August):292–300.

Haan, Frankie. 1984. Reagan: Fiscal Conservative or Carter Re-run? *Dollars and Sense,* October.

Hargrove, Erwin C., and Michael Nelson. 1984. *Presidents, Politics, and Policy.* New York: Alfred A Knopf.

Harris, Fred R., and Paul L. Hain. 1983. *America's Legislative Processes.* Glenview, IL: Scott, Foresman & Co.

Harrison, Benjamin. 1897. *This Country of Ours.* New York: Charles Scribner's Sons.

Hartz, Louis. 1955. *The Liberal Tradition in America.* New York: Harcourt, Brace & World.

Heclo, Hugh. 1977. *Studying the Presidency.* New York: Ford Foundation.

Hearn, William E. 1867. *The Government of England.* Melbourne: George Robertson.

Hill Overrides Veto of South Africa Sanctions. 1986. *Congressional Quarterly Weekly Report,* October 4.

Hinckley, Barbara. 1985. *Problems of the Presidency.* Glenview, IL: Scott, Foresman & Co.

Hobson, Charles F. 1979. The Negative on State Laws: James Madison and the Crisis of Republican Government. *William and Mary Quarterly* 36(April):215–35.

Hoff, Samuel B. 1987. Presidential Support in the Veto Process, 1889–1985. Ph.D. Diss., State University of New York at Stony Brook.

House Documents.

House Journal.

House Panels Prepare the Way for South African Sanctions Bill. 1986. *Congressional Quarterly Weekly Report,* June 14.

Jackson, Carlton. 1967. *Presidential Vetoes, 1792–1945.* Athens, GA: University of Georgia Press.

Jennings, Williams I. 1959. *Cabinet Government.* Cambridge: Cambridge University Press.

Jolowicz, Herbert F. 1967. *Historical Introduction to the Study of Roman Law.* Cambridge: Cambridge University Press.

Kass, Benny L. 1971. The Pocket Veto: An Elusive Bone of Contention. *American Bar Association Journal,* 57(October): 1033–35.

Keefe, William J., and Morris S. Ogul. 1981. *The American Legislative Process.* Englewood Cliffs, NJ: Prentice-Hall.

Keeffe, Arthur John, with John Harry Jorgenson. 1975. Solicitor General Pocket Vetoes the Pocket Veto. *American Bar Association Journal* 61(June):755–56.

Lambro, Donald. 1985. Available: A Proven Way to Reduce the Deficit. Reader's Digest, August, 40–43.

Lee, Jong. 1975. Presdiential Vetoes from Washington to Nixon. *Journal of Politics* 37(May):522–46.

LeLoup, Lance. 1980. *Budgetary Politics.* Brunswick, OH: King's Court Communications.

Leno, Janet. 1985. The Case Against the Line-Item Veto. *Common Cause Magazine,* July/August, 45.

Levine, Myron A. 1983. Tactical Constraints and Presidential Influence on Veto Overrides. *Presidential Studies Quarterly* 13:(Fall):646–50.

Light, Paul C. 1982. *The President's Agenda.* Baltimore, MD: Johns Hopkins University Press.

Lockwood, Henry C. 1884. *The Abolition of the Presidency.* New York: Worthington.

Long, John D. 1887. The Use and Abuse of the Veto Power. *The Forum* IV(November):253–67.

Lowi, Theodore J. 1964. American Business, Public Policy, Case Studies, and Political Theory. *World Politics* 16(July):677–715.

———. 1985. *The Personal President.* Ithaca, NY: Cornell University Press.

Mason, Edward C. 1890. *The Veto Power.* Boston: Ginn & Co.

Mason, Samson. 1841. Objections of the President to the Bill to Establish a Fiscal Corporation. Delivered in the House of Representatives, September 10. Washington, D.C.: *The National Intelligencer.*

Merrill, Horace S. 1957. *Bourbon Leader: Grover Cleveland and the Democratic Party.* Boston: Little, Brown.

*Messages and Papers of the Presidents. 1913.* Washington, D.C.: Bureau of National Literature.

Moe, Ronald C. 1987. The Founders and their Experience with the Executive Veto. *Presidential Studies Quarterly* 17(Spring): 413–32.

Moe, Ronald C. 1985. Prospects for the Item Veto at the Federal Level: Lessons from the States. A paper delivered at the Annual

Meeting of the American Political Science Association, New Orleans, LA, August 29–September 1.

Neustadt, Richard. 1954. Presidency and Legislation: The Growth of Central Clearance. *American Political Science Review* 48:(September):641–71.

———. 1980. *Presidential Power.* New York: Wiley.

Nevins, Allan. 1941. *Grover Cleveland: A Study in Courage.* New York: Dodd, Mead and Co.

No-Win Battle over Saudi Arms. 1986. *Time,* June 2.

O'glove, Thornton L. 1984. Vigorous Use of the Presidential Veto Power Is Needed to Control the Prolific Spending Habits of Congress. *Quality of Earnings Report* 14(September 25):175–78.

O'glove, Thornton L., and Robert Sobel. 1985. Reagan's Rhetoric and Reality Don't Agree. *The Market Chronicle,* February 21.

Ornstein, Norman J. 1985. Veto the Line Item Veto. *Fortune,* January 7, 109–11.

Palffy, John. 1984. Line-Item Veto: Trimming the Pork. *Heritage Foundation Backgrounder,* April 3.

Parker, George F. 1909. *Recollections of Grover Cleveland.* New York: The Century Co.

Paul, Ron. 1984. Minor Adjustment or Overhaul? *Ron Paul's Freedom Report,* December.

Pear, Robert. 1984. Congress's Keeper of the Constitution. *New York Times,* December 28.

Pessen, Edward. 1975. The Arrogant Veto. *The Nation,* August 30, 133–137.

Pious, Richard M. 1979. *The American Presidency.* New York: Basic Books.

Polsby, Nelson, and Aaron Wildavsky. 1980. *Presidential Elections.* New York: Charles Scribner's Sons.

Porter, Kirk H., and Donald B. Johnson, eds. 1966. *National Party Platforms.* Urbana, IL: University of Illinois Press.

Prescott, Frank W., and Joseph F. Zimmerman. 1980. *The Politics of the Veto of Legislation in New York State,* 2 vols. Washington, D.C.: University Press of America.

The President and 'Pork Barrel.' 1916. *The North American Review* 204(August):178–80.

The Presidential Veto Power: A Shallow Pocket. 1971. *Michigan Law Review* 70(November):148–70.

*Presidential Vetoes, 1789–1976.* 1978. Washington, D.C.: U.S. Government Printing Office.

*Presidential Vetoes, 1977–1984.* 1985. Washington, D.C.: U.S. Government Printing Office.

Pressure Builds for New South Africa Sanctions. 1986. *Congressional Quarterly Weekly Report,* July 26.

Private Bills in Congress. 1966. *Harvard Law Review* 79(June):1684–1706.

Pro-Israel Lobby Declines to Fight Arms Sale. 1986. *Congressional Quarterly Weekly Report,* March 29.

Proposed Saudi Missile Sale Gathers Opposition on Hill. 1986. *Congressional Quarterly Weekly Report,* April 26.

Prudential-Bache. 1984. "Washington Impact," May 21.

Pyle, Christopher H., and Richard M. Pious. 1984. *The President, Congress, and the Constitution.* New York: Free Press.

Reagan Is Seeking to Head Off Senate Action on South Africa. 1986. *Congressional Quarterly Weekly Report,* July 19.

Reinhold, Robert. 1985. Second-Guessing State Budgets, Line by Line. *New York Times,* July 28.

Renick, E. I. 1898. The Power of the President to Sign Bills after the Adjournment of Congress. *American Law Review* 32(March-April):208–20.

Reynolds, Hudson. 1985. In Favor of a Line-Item Veto. A paper delivered at the Annual Meeting of the American Political Science Association. New Orleans, LA, August 29–September 1.

Riggs, Richard A. 1973. Separation of Powers: Congressional Riders and the Veto Power. *University of Michigan Journal of Law Reform,* 6(Spring):735–59.

Ringelstein, Albert 1985. Presidential Vetoes: Motivations and Classifications. *Congress and the Presidency* 12(Spring):43–55.

Rogers, Lindsay. 1920. The Power of the President to Sign Bills After Congress Has Adjourned. *Yale Law Journal* 30(November):1–22.

Rohde, David, and Dennis M. Simon. 1985. Presidential Vetoes and Congressional Response: A Study of Institutional Conflict. *American Journal of Political Science* 29(August):397–427.

Ross, Russell M., and Fred Schwengel. 1982. An Item Veto for the President? *Presidential Studies Quarterly* 12(Winter):66–79.

Rothman, Robert. 1984. Reagan Comparatively Frugal In Exercise of His Veto Power. *Congressional Quarterly Weekly Report* (November 17):2956–57.

Senate Documents.

Serven, Abram R. 1929. The Constitution and the 'Pocket Veto.' *New York University Law Quarterly Review* 7(December): 495–508.

Shull, Steven A. 1979. *Presidential Policy Making.* Brunswick, OH: King's Court Communications.

Skowronek, Stephen. 1984. Presidential Leadership in Political Time. *The Presidency and the Political System,* ed. by Michael Nelson. Washington, D.C.: Congressional Quarterly Press.

Spitzer, Robert J. 1985. The Item Veto Reconsidered. *Presidential Studies Quarterly* 15(Summer):611–17.

_______. 1985a. The Item Veto: A Bad Idea That Lives On. *America,* June 15, 492–93.

———. 1983. *The Presidency and Public Policy.* University, AL: University of Alabama Press.

Stockman, David A. 1986. *The Triumph of Politics.* New York: Harper & Row.

Storing, Herbert J., ed. 1981. *The Complete Anti-Federalist,* 7 vols. Chicago: University of Chicago Press.

Story, Joseph. 1833. *Commentaries on the Constitution of the United States,* 3 vols. Boston: Hilliard, Gray, & Co.

Stunner in House. 1986. *Congressional Quarterly Weekly Report,* June 21.

Subcommittee on the Constitution, Judiciary Committee. 1984. Line-Item Veto. U.S. Senate, 98th Cong., 2d sess., April 9. Washington, D.C.: U.S. Government Printing Office.

Subcommittee No. 3, Committee on the Judiciary. 1957. Item Veto Hearing. U.S. House of Representatives, 85th Cong., 1st sess., May. Washington, D.C.: U.S. Government Printing Office.

Subcommittee on Separation of Powers, Committee on the Judiciary. 1971. Constitutionality of the President's 'Pocket Veto' Power. U.S. Senate, 92d Cong., 1st sess. Washington, D.C.: U.S. Government Printing Office.

Sundquist, James L. 1986. *Constitutional Reform and Effective Government.* Washington, D.C.: The Brookings Institution.

———. 1981. *The Decline and Resurgence of Congress.* Washington, D.C.: Brookings.

Symposium on the Line–Item Veto. 1985. *Notre Dame Journal of Law, Ethics, and Public Policy* 1:157–283.

Taft, William Howard. 1967. *The President and His Powers.* New York: Columbia University Press.

Taswell-Langmead, Thomas Pitt. 1946. *English Constitutional History.* Boston: Houghton Mifflin Co.

Tatalovich, Raymond, and Byron Daynes. 1984. *Presidential Power in the United States.* Monterey, CA: Brooks/Cole Publishing.

Thach, Charles C. 1969. *The Creation of the Presidency,* 1775–1789. New York: DaCapo Press.

Thomson, Harry C. 1978. The First Presidential Vetoes. *Presidential Studies Quarterly* 8(Winter):27–31.

Tocqueville, Alexis de. 1945. *Democracy in America,* 2 vols. New York: Vintage.

Towle, Katherine A. 1937. The Presidential Veto Since 1899. *American Political Science Review* 31(February):51–56.

Vandenberg, Arthur H. 1936. Hash By the Billion! Wanted: A Tax-Saving Diet. *Saturday Evening Post,* August 29, 10–11, 61–64.

The Veto Power and Kennedy v. Sampson: Burning a Hole in the President's Pocket. 1974. *Northwestern University Law Review* 69:587–625.

Vose, Clement E. 1964. The Memorandum Pocket Veto. *Journal of Politics* 26(May):397–405.

Warren, Charles. 1937. *The Making of the Constitution.* Boston: Little, Brown.

Watson, David K. 1910. *The Constitution of the United States,* 2 vols. Chicago: Callaghan & Co.

Watson, Richard A. 1987. Origins and Early Development of the Veto Power. *Presidential Studies Quarterly* 17(Spring):401–12.

Wayne, Stephen J. 1978. *The Legislative Presidency.* New York: Harper & Row.

Wayne, Stephen J., Richard L. Cole, and James F. C. Hyde, Jr. 1979. Advising the President on Enrolled Legislation. *Political Science Quarterly* 94(Summer):303–18.

Wayne, Stephen J., and James F. C. Hyde, Jr. 1978. Presidential Decision-Making on Enrolled Bills. *Presidential Studies Quarterly* 8(Summer):284–96.

Wells, Roger H. 1924. The Item Veto and State Budget Reform. *American Political Science Review* 18(November):782–91.

Wildavsky, Aaron. 1966. The Two Presidencies. *Trans-Action* (December):7–14.

Wildstrom, Stephen A. 1984. Broader Veto Power Wouldn't Help the Budget Deficit. *Business Week,* February 6.

Wilkinson, Vernon L. 1936. The Item Veto in the American Constitutional System. *Georgetown Law Journal* 25(November): 106–133.

Wilson, Woodrow. 1956. *Congressional Government.* Cleveland, OH: Meridian Books.

———. 1908. *Constitutional Government in the United States.* New York: Columbia University Press.

Witcover, Jules. 1977. *Marathon.* New York: New American Library.

Zinn, Charles J. 1951. The Veto Power of the President. U.S. Congress, House of Representatives, Committee on the Judiciary, 82d Congress, 1st sess. Washington D.C.: U.S. Government Printing Office.

Zycher, Benjamin. 1984. An Item Veto Won't Work. *Wall Street Journal,* October 24.

# ABOUT THE AUTHOR

Robert J. Spitzer is an associate professor and department chair of the Political Science Department at the State University of New York College at Cortland. He is the author of two other books, *The Presidency and Public Policy: The Four Arenas of Presidential Power* (1983), and *The Right to Life Movement and Third Party Politics* (1987). His articles have appeared in the *Journal of Politics, Policy Studies Journal, Presidential Studies Quarterly,* the *National Civic Review, America,* and various edited volumes. He is currently serving as a member of the New York State Commission on the Bicentennial of the U.S. Constitution. Spitzer received his B.A., *summa cum laude,* from SUNY College at Fredonia (1975) and his Ph.D. from Cornell University (1980).

# INDEX